MEMORIES OF HARTLEPOOL

TRUE NORTH BOOKS
DEAN CLOUGH
HALIFAX
WEST YORKSHIRE
HX3 5AX
TEL 01422 344344

THE PUBLISHERS WOULD LIKE TO THANK THE
FOLLOWING COMPANIES FOR SUPPORTING THE
PRODUCTION OF THIS BOOK

MAIN SPONSOR

F PEART & COMPANY LIMITED

JT ATKINSON & SONS LIMITED

CONTESSA CURTAINS LIMITED

GREYLIN ENGINEERING

JJ HARDY & SONS LIMITED

HARTLEPOOL ERECTION COMPANY LIMITED

HARTLEPOOL WATER PLC

HORSLEY QUENET ENGINEERING COMPANY LIMITED

H LAMB

ORDPRINT LIMITED

RICHARDSON BROS (HAULAGE) LIMITED

SILLARS ROAD CONSTRUCTION LIMITED

SUPAFLO ENGINEERING

TILLY BAILEY & IRVINE

YUILL HERITAGE HOMES LIMITED

First published in Great Britain by Crossley Book Publishing
Dean Clough
Halifax HX3 5AX
1998

© CROSSLEY BOOK PUBLISHING

ISBN 1 900 463 42 3

Introduction

Welcome to *Memories of Hartlepool*, a look back on some of the places, events and people in the town which have shaped our lives over a period of around half a century. The following pages are brought to life by the selection of images from the not-too-distant past, chosen according to their ability to rekindle memories of days gone by and show how people used to shop, work and play in the town where they grew up. Modern image reproduction techniques have enabled us to present these pictures in a way rarely seen before, and the lively design and informative text has attempted to set the book apart from some of the other works available. The chosen period is one which contains events within the memory of a large number of people in Hartlepool - this is not a book about crinolines or bowler-hats! Neither is *Memories of Hartlepool* a work of local history in the normal sense of the term. It has far more to do with entertainment than serious study, but we expect you will agree it is none the worse for that. We hope that the following pages will prompt readers' own memories of Hartlepool from days gone by - and we are always delighted to hear from people who can add to the information contained in the captions so that we can enhance future reprints of the book. Many local companies and organisations have allowed us to study their archives and include their history - and fascinating reading it makes too. The present-day guardians of the companies concerned are proud of their products, the achievements of their people and the hard work of their forefathers whose efforts created these long established firms in the first place. We are pleased to play our part by making it possible for them to share their history with a wider audience.

A 1960s scene with St. George's Church in the distance

When we began compiling *Memories of Hartlepool* several months ago we anticipated that the task would be a pleasurable one, but our expectations were greatly surpassed. There is a growing appetite for all things 'nostalgic' and we are pleased to have played a small part in swelling the number of images and associated information available to the growing number of enthusiasts.

There is much talk in modern times about the regeneration of the local economy, the influx of new industries and the challenge of attracting new enterprise from other regions to the town. And quite right too. We could, however, make the mistake of thinking that the changes are all happening *now,* but the reality is that there have always been major developments going on in the area. 'Change' is relentless and the photographs on the pages of the book serve to remind us of a mere a selection of them. Some of the images fall outside the qualification we describe as 'within living memory', but most of these will be familiar to us, either because they concern an event described to us by a close relative, or they feature monuments such as the businesses or buildings we simply felt compelled to mention. Whatever the view taken on the boundaries which separate 'history', 'nostalgia' and the present time, we should all invest a few moments occasionally to reflect on the past and the events which made our town what it is today.

Memories of Hartlepool has been a pleasure to compile, we sincerely hope you enjoy reading it.

Happy memories!

TEXT	PHIL HOLLAND
COVER DESIGN/PHOTOGRAPH COMPILATION	MARK SMITH
DESIGNERS	MANDY WALKER AND CHRISTINE GALE
BUSINESS DEVELOPMENT EDITOR	ANDREW HALES
COPYWRITER	SARAH PARKS

CONTENTS

Around the town centre

The undeniably distinctive facade of M. Robinson and Sons' Lynn Street store as it appeared to passers-by in October 1966. The style of Liverpool House was not to everyone's taste but the goods on offer behind the massive shop windows certainly were.

Towns normally judge which is their premier shopping street according to where the *big names* of British retailing choose to locate their stores.

Marks and Spencer, F.W Woolworth and Boots are among the main ones in mind, and if this was the criterion Lynn Street would definitely have been considered the number one shopping street at the time this picture was taken. All the big retailers had branches here right up until the time it was demolished, making Lynn Street the place to buy everything from food to clothing, and from televisions to headache tablets.

Stranton Post Office dominates the shops in this view of Vicarage Gardens. The picture dates from 1966 and other well-known shops at this time included Jean's flower shop, Ashtons tobacconists and M. Pickering's the grocers. The substantial properties were built on three storeys with an unusual blend of mock tudor and brickwork. Most of the shopkeepers lived above the properties in the spacious living accommodation contained there. The shops were built on the site of an

orchard in the care of the Vicar of Stranton in the first half of the 19th century. The vicar was noted for his kind deeds, one being to distribute the fruit grown in his orchard to the poor. This fine parade of shops was named after the vicarage garden upon which it stands. This picture was taken in November, as a year which saw the triumph of England's World Cup win and the despair of the Aberfan disaster, in which 116 children and 28 adults lost their lives, drew quietly to a close.

Above: A delightfully-nostalgic single-decker bus approaches the camera having just passed Barclays Bank. The bus reminds us of a time when our public transport vehicles seemed to have real character, and we wonder if this method of getting around would be more popular if they looked this attractive today. The church clock was showing 11.40 am. This picture affords a good view of the Old Municipal Buildings on the left of the picture with several characterful motor saloons parked outside. Notice the statue of Ralph Ward Jackson - the man said to be responsible for putting West Hartlepool 'on the map' - just visible outside the church. Ralph Ward Jackson made the building of Christ Church possible. It was a proud day for him when it opened in 1854. Two years earlier the Athenaeum opened on Church Street, funds being raised by public subscription and a large donation by Ward Jackson. Christ Church went on to play a useful role as a magnificent art gallery. The delightful Old Municipal Buildings, shown just left of centre became prestigious offices in later years.

Below: This 1970 scene shows a point-duty policeman hard at work at the junction of Clarence Road and Church Street.

The picture dates from barely three decades before the compilation of this book, and as such this would be one of the last opportunities to witness this form of routine traffic control before it was phased out altogether. As an aid to visibility the officer is wearing white arm bands and white gloves, as well as standing on a yellow and black cubicle designed to raise the public servant a few more inches higher than the passing motorists. Well before the era featured here it was usual that point duty officers would work at the same road junction as a matter of routine. In doing so they would become well-known to regular users of the highway and a rapport would be built over a period of years. Of course, when traffic lights were introduced the need for point duty policemen diminished, releasing the officers for other duties.

Above: Scenes like this one showing a patch of cleared land in the centre of Hartlepool were commonplace in the post war era. The photograph was taken in June 1965.

Right: The pleasing design of Borough Buildings made it one of the areas treasures ever since it opened in 1889, just two years after the granting of the Charter of Incorporation to West

It was typical at this time for open land awaiting development to be used as a temporary car park, this being the time before multi-storey car parks seemed to stand on every street corner. In the distance, to the right, a sign indicates the location of the Royal Vaults.

WEST HARTLEPOOL WAS GRANTED THE CHARTER OF INCORPORATION IN 1887

Hartlepool. This picture was taken in March 1966 on what was obviously a quiet day judging by the half-empty car park and light sprinkling of pedestrians. Many examples of the cars featured here have survived until the present day more than three decades later. A sign on the side of the

Buses seem to be parked almost haphazardly on the area to the left, reminding us of the livery that public transport vehicles carried before the *Hartlepools* were amalgamated - the old Borough decked out in a lovely shade of blue and West Hartlepool's buses in a distinctive red livery.

Borough Buildings indicates the location of the local housing office. This housing office would come to have a special significance in the years to follow, as large numbers of houses were to be swept away with the creation of the new central shopping area. Less than a year after the picture was taken the two *Hartlepools* combined to create a unified borough.

Few people have seen Church Street from this viewpoint. And no wonder, for the picture was taken from high above that familiar Hartlepool Street from the tower of Christ Church. Two successful high street banks dominate this end of Church Street; Lloyds Bank with its three floors and georgian windows can be seen on the right. On the opposite side of the street the rival Barclays branch stands only a short walk away. Large zebra crossings, complete with belisha beacons, provide a safe passage between the two. As a point of interest, belisha beacons took their name from the Minister of Transport at the time of the 1930 Road Traffic Act, Mr Hore Belisha M.P. Church Street owed much to the prestigious shops and businesses which served Hartlepool people from this location over many years, including Blacketts (formerly Hill and Carter), the Commercial Hotel and Birks Cafe. The area suffered damage during the last war from enemy bombing raids.

Below: The delightful lamp standard alone make this photograph a 'must' for inclusion in the book, reminding us of how elegant some of Hartlepool 'street furniture' was in days gone by. This picture dates from December 1966 and it was taken in the Northgate area of Hartlepool. Several memorable businesses can be seen along what was once a thriving commercial part of the town. The Globe Hotel was a *Vaux* house, standing on the corner of Northgate and Cleveland Street. Nearer the camera the pawn-broking business owned by Blooms looks as if it had seen much better days than this and Pools Dyeworks' shop next door is well and truly boarded up. In the distance a poster site advertises Cadets cigarettes with the slogan 'Give Cadets, the NOW cigarettes with gifts.'

Bottom: The imposing four storey retail premises which was the home of Blacketts store for decades. The picture dates from the early 1960s and shows around twenty shoppers hurrying between Church Street and Whitby Street, obviously unaware of the photographer recording the scene.

More mature readers may remember that the store once went under the name of Hill-Carters, responsible for supplying the furniture for many of the homes in Hartlepool over many years. In more recent times it became the home of the Dovecot

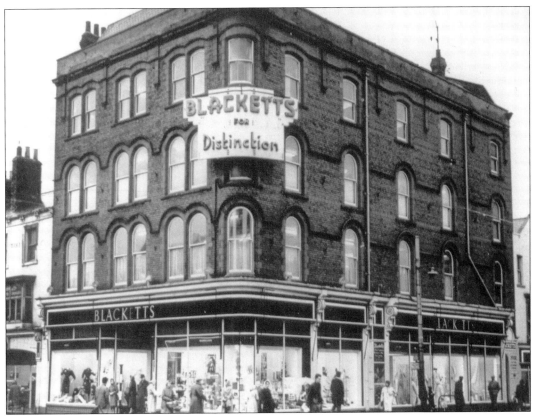

A late 1960s view of the shops along Lynn Street shows only a handful of shoppers and one or two elderly motorcars in an area which was normally a hive of activity. The picture is dominated by Market Buildings, a narrow gated entrance in which led to a bustling indoor market full of enticing sights, sounds and aromas capable of turning the head of any hardened shopper. Across the way from Market Buildings was the Market Hotel, a Vaux house and a favourite haunt of serious drinkers in town-centre Hartlepool. The sign marking the location of the Empire is just visible in the distance, on the right. This street was also the home of Marks and Spencers, Woodhouses and Hardy's furniture retailers, Boots the chemists and the Singer sewing machine shop. Sewing shops supplied machines, either electrically or treadle operated, along with cotton, needles, zips, buttons, patterns and everything else needed by the home dressmaker.

Of course, the adjacent market was very conveniently positioned for those wishing to buy material to make clothes at home. The trade in these items would tend to be seasonal, with a rush being experienced when housewives and mothers were busy making clothes for some religious festival or holiday, Christmas and public holiday times.

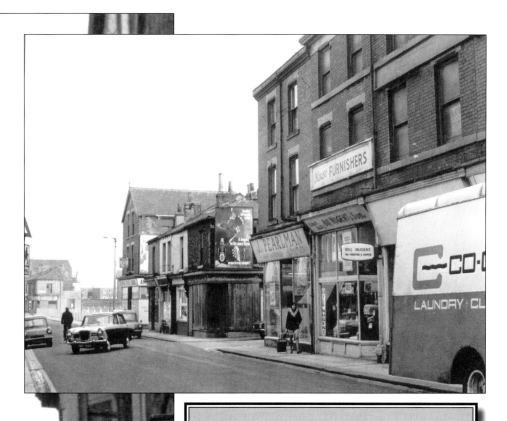

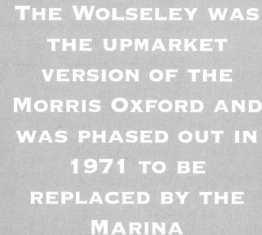

THE WOLSELEY WAS THE UPMARKET VERSION OF THE MORRIS OXFORD AND WAS PHASED OUT IN 1971 TO BE REPLACED BY THE MARINA

Above: This view along Musgrove Street dates from January 1971. Several well-known shops are featured, including Bill Nugent's Furniture and Carpets who were advertising a sale at the time. A Wolseley 16/60 was pulling out into the main road when the photographer released his shutter. This classy motor was the up-market version of the Morris Oxford/Austin Cambridge saloon, its leather interior and re-styled front end being the major differences. All versions were phased out around 1971 and replaced by the lack-lustre Marina range. Still on a motoring theme, two Ford Anglia vans with their stark 'expressions' are pointed in the direction of the camera. There are very few of these remaining today, most suffering badly from corrosion problems and later superseded by the *Escort* range of vans from 1968 onwards.

At leisure

Left: The distinctive grey outline of St. George's church can be seen at the junction of Park Road and York Road. The late 1960s scene is given atmosphere by the cars parked beside the thriving shops along this busy route. They serve as reference points to focus our sense of time, in much the same way as signposts help our sense of direction.

The Triumph Spitfire sports car was the object of many a young man's dreams, but dad would have preferred the light-coloured Hillman Minx saloon behind it, or the star of ITV's 'Z' Cars, the Ford Zephyr, parked outside the shop on the corner. Coverdale's sold typewriters and office requirements from the shop in the centre of the picture. Further along the street was a central heating showroom next door to a television shop. Televisions and central heating were 'on the up' when this picture was taken... which is more than could be said about the long-term prospects for typewriters!

Below: West Hartlepool's Gray Art Gallery and Museum conservatory was the setting for this delightful photograph which dates from the early 1950s. The smartly-dressed young couple are admiring the impressive selection of potted plants - common in most garden/DIY centres of today but considered exotic half a century ago. The much-admired marble statues located here were known as 'Innocence' and 'Suzanne and the Elders.' The Gray family had built a large fortune in Hartlepool through their success in the shipbuilding industry. In addition to acquiring large country estates at several locations the family had a track record locally of supporting worthy causes with their wealth. The Gray Art Gallery and Museum was once the home of Sir William Gray who arrived in West Hartlepool in 1843 from Blyth in Northumberland.

Among his achievements Gray was twice mayor of Hartlepool and more than two decades later was elected the first Mayor of West Hartlepool.

An elevated view of Croft Gardens which shows how they appeared almost half a century ago. The proximity of the tranquil gardens to the sea is clear from this photograph. Fresh sea breezes characterised the gardens in all but the warmest weather.

The design of the gardens was the work of Hartlepool's Borough Engineer and Surveyor Mr R H Snowball. The gentle curves and broad areas of perfectly smooth lawns combined to create an unrivalled sense of calm and peacefulness.

EMPIRE THEATRE
West Hartlepool

WEEK COMMENCING MONDAY, NOVEMBER 15th, 1948
6.15 — TWICE NIGHTLY — 8.30

LEAP YEAR REVELS

GIRLS, GLAMOUR and GAIETY

DAVY KAYE

THE B.B.C.'s NEW STAR COMEDIAN

HAZEL WILSON
ENGLAND'S NEW SINGING SENSATION

DON ARROL
A NUT IN THE HUT

ZENA KYNOCH
SOUBRETTE

IVOR HUGHES
BARITONE

HARRY RUTHERFORD

LANE-HOLLEY TRIO
MUSIC WITH A DIFFERENCE

MOLLY JAMES
COMEDIENNE

TONY & SHEILA
2 SMART GIRLS

CHICK REVILL
YOUTH, PEP AND PERSONALITY

THE LEAP YEAR LOVELIES

THE THREE KARLOFFS
EXTRAORDINARY GIFTS

TAYLORS THEATRICAL PRINTERS, WOMBWELL, YORKS

Above: West Hartlepool's Empire Theatre served a willing audience between 1909 and 1959. During this period spanning half a century audiences were treated to a combination of review, pantomime, theatre and even opera. All the big names appeared here, ranging from Morecambe and Wise to Jimmy

Jewel. The interior of the Empire was luxurious by the standards of the overwhelming majority of people and kitted out in extremely ornate Renaissance style with lots of plaster figures and columns sprouting from the walls and ceilings. This advertisement from November 1948 was one of the many ways used by the management of the theatre to attract customers. By this time of course there was intense competition between this 'old-style' form of entertainment and the burgeoning number of cinemas in the district. Sadly the Empire was to loose the battle, and close less than a decade after this notice was published.

Top: Croft Gardens as they appeared in 1950, as planting out was nearing completion. The gardens provided a tranquil oasis of space where local people could relax and enjoy a moment or two of peace and quiet in a beautiful setting close to St Hilda's church and the centre of Hartlepool. The gardens took their name from the *Croft* an area of land between the market place and the sea which was home to people who made their livings from the sea. The quality of the housing stock here was mixed, and the area had more than its fair share of damp, insanitary dwellings which were removed in the late 1930s. This scene is dominated by the Borough Buildings municipal offices and the much newer semi-detached property housing Verrill's popular fish and chip shop.

The fashions of the early 1940s are evident in this picture. Not that fashion was uppermost in people's minds at this time. Something had caused the group - mainly of men and children - to gather on the Bell Street. There is more than a whiff of curiosity at the presence of a photographer, particularly but not exclusively among the children in the foreground. It is possible that the crowds were out in 1940 as a result of the Hartlepools experiencing their first air raid of the Second World War.

That sad event took place on June 19th 1940 and two people lost their lives. This was one of the first bombing raids on Britain during the conflict. Churchill had been appointed Prime Minister just a month before, and the outlook for the nation was dark and uncertain.

Wartime

Above: There is a sharp contrast in this picture between the normality of everyday life as represented by the lady pushing her pram near Brenda Road, and the sheer devastation caused by a Nazi bomb just a few feet away. Perhaps 'keeping up appearances' was one way of coping with the chaos and showing the world that we couldn't be intimidated by anything the enemy could throw at us. Hartlepool people had bravery in abundance - and they needed it, for there were almost 500 air-raid warnings during the conflict and more than 40 actual raids where bombs fell on the twin towns. This scene depicts the aftermath of the raid on West Hartlepool on August 26 1940, a time when the *Battle of Britain* was raging in the skies. Britain and her brave airmen prevailed; three weeks after this photograph was taken Hitler abandoned his plan to invade Britain, convinced that the RAF was too strong for Germany's Luftwaffe.

Above right: 'Stick to Beer, for Beer is Best' proclaimed the smiling face on the poster outside the Central Hotel. But there was little to smile about for the people of West Hartlepool on the day that this picture was taken. The picture shows the damage caused to the public house by falling bombs on the night of June 20th 1940. Around 250 properties were damaged in this heavy raid which claimed two lives within a short distance of the Central Hotel. The issue of gas masks had already taken place by the time this picture was taken. Every man woman and child was required to carry one at all times, the fear being that poisonous gas would be used on the civilian population in much the same way as it was used on troops during the First War. In the event there was never any gas attack on British soil. The allocation of domestic and public air-raid shelters had a more practical effect on the drive to minimise casualties - and with the record of bombardment in the area local people took very little persuading to use them.

The remains of the once-proud houses in the Musgrave Street area after the bombing raid of 19th June 1940 are surveyed by a police officer and two Council officials. Two workmen can just be seen struggling with something near the pavement - perhaps they were isolating a gas or water main to prevent further disruption. The interior walls of two of the dwellings are left open to the elements, not that much more damage could be done than had already been sustained. What is surprising is that three pictures can be seen hanging on the remaining walls of the houses, despite the massive blast that had destroyed everything else. Perhaps that was why the policeman was standing with hands on hips as an unconscious expression of his shock and disbelief.

Above: Curious residents stood on their steps to watch the progress being made by some hard-working road layers. This was Bell Street in Central Estate, in the late 1930s, and the workmen were spreading stone chippings on a thin layer of tar put down by the slow moving lorry seen in the distance. Pedestrians are wisely using the opposite side of the road to avoid the sticky mess underfoot. The shop in the distance was a grocers and general dealers owned by Newton Watson. On the opposite side of the street was a barbers' shop which also sold tobacco and sweets which was owned by Tommy Newton. At the end of the street it is just possible to make out the outline of the timber yards to the rear of Cleveland Road.

Scenes like this remind us of days gone by when there was a greater sense of community in our towns and suburbs. These were times when people really did leave their doors unlocked without the fear of unwelcome visitors - not that there would have been much to steal in any case. These days many people know the characters on television soap operas better than they know their own neighbours - and our communities are all the worse for that.

Left: The depressing sight of houses reduced to a crumpled heap of matchwood and broken bricks was the result of a bombing raid on 30th August 1940. There was a danger from falling masonry as surviving householders picked through the remains of their houses in a bid to salvage clothes, furniture, food and personal items from the chaotic scene that faced them. In cases such as this the chances of saving anything useful from the wreckage were slim indeed, but that didn't stop people from trying. The *Hartlepools* importance as a port, shipbuilding and steel producing centre made it an attractive target to the German raiders. The R.A.F presence at Greatham airport (1939 - 1947) was a comfort in some ways but another reason for the enemy to visit too. Throughout the Second World War Hartlepool was a regular target for the bombers, and in all around 7500 separate properties were damaged and seventy people lost their lives.

A scene of utter devastation met residents of Musgrave Street and the surrounding houses when they emerged from their air-raid shelters after a bombing raid in June 1942. A direct-hit had reduced the 'houses' in the foreground to a pile of rubble and broken roof beams. The private, carefully cleaned and decorated domestic interiors were now laid bare for all to see. A sight capable of reducing once proud housewives and their sympathetic neighbours to tears. Surrounding houses escaped the direct full force of the nazi bomb but had slates and windows destroyed by the incredible force of the blast. Dust and broken glass was everywhere, both inside and outside the shattered dwellings. Bricks, slates and huge pieces of masonry had been hurled hundreds of yards through windows and slated roofs to become embedded in precious wardrobes, sideboards and pianos inside. Mains services such as water and gas were disrupted. Workmen struggled to isolate leaks and repair the damage - as shown here with the men in the foreground - and everyone 'pulled together' in true wartime spirit.

Above: A sense of shock and disbelief hit the residents of West Hartlepool's Faulder Street after the air raid of 26 August 1940. One house, shown here had taken a direct hit, and rooftops, windows and masonry was damaged over an extensive distance.

The sad sight of personal belongings piled up on the street is evident; anything that could be salvaged was taken away with the displaced residents to the homes of friends and relatives until somewhere permanent could be found. This had been a heavy raid; bombs had fallen on the beach and on Church Street. The Yorkshire Penny Bank, the Clarence Hotel and Edgar Phillip's shop nearby were severely damaged and had to be pulled down.

Right: The *Hartlepools* endured the effects of the German bombing campaign, with all the worry and terrific disruption that went with it, for a period lasting just short of three years. The first raid on the area took place on June 19th 1940 and the last on March 22nd 1943. Such was the damage sustained by *the Hartlepools* that Prime Minister Winston Churchill made an official morale-boosting visit to the area, flying into the RAF base at Greathams. This scene was very typical of the aftermath of a German raid; houses damaged beyond repair by the tremendous force of a direct hit, and adjacent properties left tottering on their cracked founda-tions. Many seemingly-repairable properties had to be pulled down because they were considered dangerous and unsafe.

HARLAND & PARKER
BUILDERS
DECORATORS
2 YORK RD

THE PARISH CHURCH OF St LUKE
WEST HARTLEPOOL
TO THE GLORY OF GOD
THIS STONE WAS LAID BY
Mrs G. J. B. BIDGOOD
WIFE OF THE FIRST VICAR
JUNE 8TH 1932

Events & occasions

THE FOUNDATIONS OF THE PARISH CHURCH OF ST LUKE IN WEST HARTLEPOOL WERE LAID IN JUNE 1932

This magnificent group photograph was taken to commemorate the laying of the foundation stone for the Parish Church of St. Luke in West Hartlepool. Remarkably, it dates from June 1932. The stone was laid by Mrs G.B. Bidgood, the wife of the first Vicar. She can be seen to the right of the large, white inscribed stone which is suspended by the sturdy wooden gantry. Within the steel framework of the growing structure a party of religious and civic dignitaries, raised above the level of the rest of the gathering stand beneath the shrewdly-positioned advertising sign for Harland and Parker 'builders and decorators' of York Road. One striking aspect of the picture is the clothing being worn by the people shown. The ladies are wearing the fashionable tight-fitting hats from the day with fur collars and a few fox-stoles in evidence.

It is difficult to find any lady without some form of head-covering, and most of the men are *equipped* with a hat even if they are not wearing one at the moment.

LINGFORDS' BAKING POWDER

Top: *Little is known for certain about this photograph but circumstantial evidence suggests that it was taken at an exhibition at one of the Hartlepools civic buildings, probably during the 1930s. The stand was constructed to promote the use of Lingfords' baking powder. These were the days when it was almost unheard of for housewives to buy ready made cakes and pastries, and home baking took up many hours of each week. A sign above the stand encourages visitors to ask for a free sample, and another welcomes trade enquiries. The free samples were actually an assortment of mouthwatering cakes and buns, all made with the magic baking powder on offer at the exhibition. One notice informs potential customers that the two sponges on display were made with ingredients costing 6 1/2d (less than 3p). Those were the days!*

Above: *Many readers will be familiar with the image of Sir William Gray, who was one of Hartlepool's leading industrialists when this photograph was taken. The picture marks the occasion of the launching of the S.S Degema at Gray's Central Yard in 1958. Sir William is shown carefully handing the traditional bottle of 'bubbly' to Mrs P. Arundale the wife of the managing director of Elder Dempster Lines, the owners of the vessel. Looking on is a youthful Kathleen Copping who later presented Mrs Arundale with a bouquet of flowers.*

An historic photograph featuring the last meeting of Hartlepool Council in 1967. The Mayor, Cllr. D. Waller, stands proudly in the middle of his civic officials for the occasion to be recorded. There had been talk of the merger of the two Hartlepools for as long as most people could remember.
Despite all the anxiety and perceived rivalry that had existed between the authorities the transformation went through smoothly.

And so it was, that on April 1st 1967 that the ancient Borough of Hartlepool and the County Borough of West Hartlepool became one.
From the time of the amalgamation several peripheral villages were included in the new authority making it larger than before. There were widespread celebrations throughout the area lasting several weeks. What had once been considered unthinkable had now happened.

The oil and timber firm...

The park and garden furniture produced by F Peart & Company is the creation of craftsmen who use only the finest quality plantation-grown teak. Teak is one of the world's most valuable woods. Hard, heavy and strong, it has natural properties which help it to withstand the elements and is almost immune to decay.

Harvesting the teak trees in areas such as Java, where machinery is rare, is a labour-intensive business. A strip of bark and sapwood is removed from the tree before it is left for 2-3 years to die and dry. Eventually the trees are cut down with handsaws and transported from the forest by bullocks. Then, via trucks and the forest railway, the teak is transported to its shipping point.

Once inside the Peart factory, the teak is skillfully cut and shaped into the component parts of the company's wide range of park and garden furniture designs. Each item of furniture is hand-built by experienced craftsmen with an eye for detail and concern for outstanding quality of finish.

No nails are used in the construction process, and screws are carefully concealed with teak plugs. Mortice and tenon joints, strengthened with glue and teak dowels, are typical of the traditional methods employed.

This care about the quality of company products leads to the sheer comfort that is the end product of meticulous research and stringent testing of all designs.

Fred Peart started the company in 1923, he put everything he had into the company with a bulk of the capital provided by his wife. The company started as coal and coke merchants and the business grew rapidly. The initial horses and carts that were used to haul the products during the early years were slowly replaced by motor transport in the early 1930's. Using these vehicles

Above: Fred Peart, the founder of the company.
Below: A view of the automated coal bagging plant installed in the mid-1960's.

with a variety of tips and end sections, both uncreosoted and pressure creosoted. Wire fencing was made with different meshes for cattle, sheep and pigs. An all-welded nine feet steel field gate cost 72s 6d. Tubular steel was more expensive. A ten foot gate cost £7 17s 0d.

Already park and garden seats were being made. Item 474 is an octagonal tree seat made in sections. For an inner diameter of 3ft the price was £50 16s 2d. Tennis court fencing was made in a range of gauges.

By the early sixties the company's catalogue

during the quieter summer months to haul pit props to his suppliers of coal, Fred Peart learned about the timber trade. This knowledge was used in the late 40's when the company started to deal in timber and fencing products with the post war demand being tremendous. Coal sales were the mainstay of the fuel business until the early 1970's when the company's oil division began to takeover.

In 1925 Fred Peart took the brave step of setting up a limited company in very unsettled times. King George 5th reigned over a vast British Empire but the nation was still recovering from the effects of one world war, unaware that another one loomed. The economic climate was unpredictable and the commercial environment harsh. Even though the worst of the Depression was soon to arrive, the Pearts' company was modestly successful from the very first. It had two telephone lines when Hartlepool subscribers numbered under ten thousand. In addition to the supply of fencing, the company carried out erection work, on large and small scales. They accepted work from architects, surveyors, building and public works contractors, 'municipalities', including county councils, together with public authorities and national corporations.

A catalogue from the early fifties describes the company as 'specialists in fencing erection' and offers timber, steel and concrete fencing. Timber fencing posts were offered

begins with an apology that it cannot contain all the ranges the company supplied. The firm's Motor Transport fleet is proudly announced. It delivered fencing to all parts of the country but erection work was confined mainly to the north eastern parts of England.

The customer was required to order intelligently. "Is the excavation for post holes," he is asked, "in a reasonable type soil? If heavier than London clay, full details as to formation should be given."

Above: A gathering of friends and colleagues, some of them on leave during the Second World War.
Below: In the early 1970s one of Peart's oil tankers.

The Drivall was the company's answer to 'Fencer's fatigue'. The secret of the 'miracle post driver' lay in the Drivall's piston principle which concentrated maximum power in the head of the post. Hand operated by one or more men according to the size of the post they were working with, this remarkable new tool needed no motor. The well known broadcaster Roy Hay gave the Drivall his wholehearted approval.

During the 1960s, electric fencing formed part of Peart's stock. Garden seats - one of the company's ongoing line, were much more ornamental, and in this particular catalogue the 'rustic' style was very much in vogue.

After the death of Fred Peart in 1962, John Peart, Fred's eldest son made the decision to move the company offices from Park and York Road Corner, Hartlepool to

the Baltic Works, Baltic Street where the company telephone had three lines.

Wooden palisade fencing was advertised as conforming to British Standard Specification 1722 Part 6 of 1951. The layman seldom realises that these simple domestic objects have to comply with government regulations as well as the demands of the customer.

Vandals were raising their ugly heads and barbed wire concertinas 'To the very latest UK Ministry of Defence specification" appeared, offered for both civilian and military use. They were made of super high tensile spring steel wire, three times the strength of ordinary barbed wire and very difficult to cut, they were dipped in a special bitumen compound for long life under adverse conditions. Other new entries in a new catalogue included crash barrier fencing for the central reservations on motorways and galvanised wire mesh litter baskets.

By the eighties the range of contract work the company had carried out included the fencing of oil refineries, wild life safari parks, chemical installations, bird sanctuaries, factories and power stations. Park furniture by now included mild steel tree guards and concrete paving has moved into glorious technicolour, offered in red, buff, green, marigold, black and white.

In 1993 the company launched into the mass production of steel corrugated pale security fencing. This strengthened job security for the existing workforce as it increased the manufacturing capabilities for the fencing division.

In 1994 F Peart & Company bought a depot in Blyth in a major strategic move to service clients in the Tyneside and Northumberland area. It consisted of five storage tanks for road diesel, gas oil and kerosene, covering marine, industrial, agricultural and domestic customers. The purchase strengthened the company's workforce which grew to 85.

In 1997 the company announced a major expansion to its business with a view to making it the largest independent oil distributor in the north east. Having merged with Jarrow-based distributor and heating engineers Thermofuels, they achieved a 30% increase in sales and an increase in turnover of approximately £7 million. Twenty new staff were taken on and the company's strategy for the nineties has been to continue and expand its business in the north east, offering a broader and better range of services across that region. There has been a corresponding increase in the size of fleet to allow greater flexibility and quicker delivery times.

This family-owned business is now in its third generation and is celebrating its 75th anniversary this year. It occupies a twelve-acre manufacturing and storage site from which it supplies clients' needs all over

Left: Pearts make their contribution to the Coronation celebration's.

the UK and into Europe. Throughout the years F Peart & Company Ltd have become synonymous with the production and supply of all types of fencing and associated products, using timber, steel and concrete. Goods are supplied either in standard design or tailor made to individual specifications.

The company also manufactures its own range of steel corrugated pale fencing. This is recognised as the ultimate in steel security fencing for today's climate of crime and vandalism. Products are in accordance with British Standards. The teak garden and park furniture is still continuing to enhance the company's reputation.

Peart's oil fuel and lubricants division retails and distributes to a broad spectrum customer base. This is within the marine, agricultural, domestic and industrial sectors between Thirsk and the borders and across to the Pennines. They are also distributors for leading names such as Elf, Castrol, Mobil, Esso and Peart's own high quality brand.

Impressively, the family owned business has an extensive fleet of road tankers and is the largest distributor of fuel oils in the North East of England.

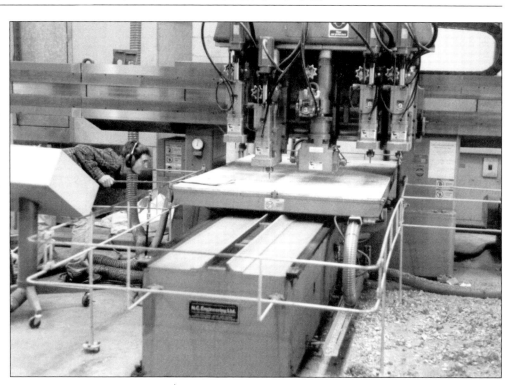

The company is the largest Authorised Distributor for Phillips Petroleum, an American oil company, with a refinery on the Tees. The company also has a depot in Blyth, Northumberland, which caters for consumers based north of the Tyne. Peart's Boiler Maintenance Division services oil and gas systems as well as carrying out boiler and central heating installations.

The current board comprises the late Mr Fred Peart's youngest son David, who is Chairman, and Jonathon and Freddie Peart, the founder's grandsons who are directors. David's son Roger is poised to join the family firm in the near future on leaving his present position as an oil trader in London.

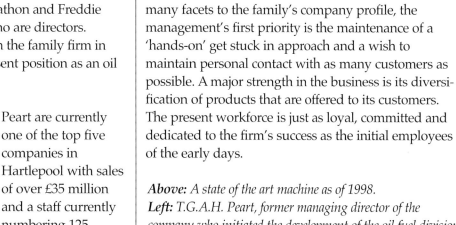

Peart are currently one of the top five companies in Hartlepool with sales of over £35 million and a staff currently numbering 125. Despite the passage of time, changing technology, external influences, the acquisition of additional companies and the many facets to the family's company profile, the management's first priority is the maintenance of a 'hands-on' get stuck in approach and a wish to maintain personal contact with as many customers as possible. A major strength in the business is its diversification of products that are offered to its customers. The present workforce is just as loyal, committed and dedicated to the firm's success as the initial employees of the early days.

Above: A state of the art machine as of 1998.
Left: T.G.A.H. Peart, former managing director of the company who initiated the development of the oil fuel division in the 1960s. ***Bottom left:*** *Aerial view of F. Peart & Co as it is today.* ***Bottom right:*** *The board in 1992. Jonathon Peart, John Peart, (the then Chairman), Freddie Peart and the current Chairman, David Peart.* ***Facing page top left:*** *J.H. Peart, who worked for the company for nearly fifty years, developed the timber and fencing division of the company and was also Chairman from 1962 until 1993.* ***Facing page top right:*** *At work in the metal shop in the 1960's.* ***Facing page bottom:*** *Industrial concrete fencing in the course of erection in the 1950's.*

Bird's eye view

Below: This photograph dates from the late 1940s and shows a view of Hartlepool long before it was transformed by the construction of the Middleton Grange Shopping Centre. The foreground of the picture is dominated by All Saints Church at Stranton, just the shortest of walks away from the 1852 Lion Brewery which was built by William Waldon. Waldon died shortly after the brewery was completed and the business eventually passed into the hands of a trusted employee by the name of *Cameron*.

The rest, as they say, is history. Stockton Street is the broad thoroughfare running across the bottom of the picture. Roughly opposite the brewery stood a popular cinema. Probably known by readers as the *Gaumont* it was originally the Picture House when opened in 1920.

This was the first local cinema to show a 'talking' film, a very well supported event which took place in 1929. Keen eyes may just be able to make out the outline of the War Memorial in the distance.

Right: Some distinctive shapes confirm this location as the Headland, with the Victoria Dock at the top of the picture. The paraphernalia associated with the dock, such as the old coal staithes (later removed), adjacent timber yards and buildings supporting the local fishing industry are clearly visible. On the extreme left of the picture the old Northgate Railway Station (it would later be demolished in the mid 1960s) can also be seen. Nearby it is possible to discern the shape of the roof of the North East Co-op building. Rows of terraced houses and the more modern dwellings in the picture, were once the homes of the workers and sailors associated with maritime activities.

A September 1967 aerial view, taken from a single-engined 'plane flying at 1200 feet, shows most of the best-known landmarks in the area to good effect. Almost in the centre of the scene is the distinctive outline of Christ Church with Church Street before it. The right hand edge of the picture is framed by the railway lines which served commercial and passenger traffic alike. At the top right of the photograph the sports ground and floodlit soccer pitch is shown, with stock piles of wood awaiting shipment beneath it. It is likely that the reason this picture was commissioned had much to do with the forthcoming construction of the Middleton Grange shopping centre. Land had already been cleared adjacent to Stockton Street ready for the serious work to begin.
Slightly lower down from that point is the distinctive roof of the College of Further Education.

Left: Changes were afoot which would see the end of shipbuilding in the area and the decline of Hartlepool's activities as a port when this scene was captured in 1964. Perhaps that was the reason the picture was taken? The breakwater can be seen, as straight as an arrow at the bottom of the picture, as can the Old Pier and lighthouse to the left of it. The Croft and St. Hilda's Church are clearly in view, as is the War Memorial in the foreground on the promenade. Behind Hartlepool Headland the intricate shapes of the dock area are shown; Victoria Dock, the Fish quay and Old Harbour in the distance. We are struck by the sight of so many houses clustered together in various parts of the picture; they look very vulnerable to the effects of the weather and the sea from this angle.

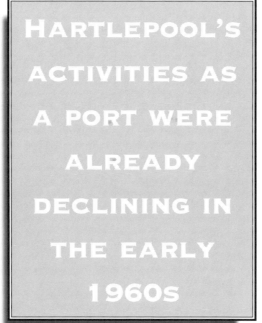

HARTLEPOOL'S ACTIVITIES AS A PORT WERE ALREADY DECLINING IN THE EARLY 1960s

Below: A spectacular, map-like view of Hartlepool Docks as they appeared around three decades before the time of writing, in the late 1960s. In the far distance the coastline can be seen with the Headland, substantial Coal Staithes and Victoria Dock quite nearby. The centre of the picture is dominated by the broad expanse of water which made up the Jackson Dock, Coal Dock and Union Dock. To the left of these major landmarks a reminder of the once-mighty shipbuilding industry takes the form of William Grays shipyard offices, just discernable at the edge of the precisely defined outline of Swainson Dock. From here, towards the top of the picture there is evidence of Hartlepool's function as a large-scale timber importer. On the other side of Swainson Dock it is possible to make out the buildings which go to make up the railway station.

A late 1960s view of Hartlepool showing construction work on the Middleton Grange Shopping Centre approaching its final stages. Victory Square and the cenotaph are clearly visible behind the shopping centre, with Victoria Road and the Civic Centre a short distance to the right. At the top right hand side of the picture the Wesley Chapel can be seen with Church Street and Christ Church lower down. Almost in the centre of the view is the College of Further Education with Stockton Street nearby and the old Co-op building to the left of them. The picture gives an impression of just how many wide open spaces there were in this part of the district, especially in the foreground where relatively new residential flats have been built.

This largely light-industrial scene was captured from a height of 1500 feet, looking from the direction of Hartlepool Bay towards Stranton. At the top of the picture it is possible to make out the course of Stockton Street and see the old Co-op building and the distinctive twin white towers on top of the *Picture House* (which later became the *Gaumont* before its inevitable conversion to a bingo hall). All Saints Church at Stranton and the substantial works of Cameron's Brewery are also in view. The left hand side of the photograph features the long curving Burn Road with Baltic Street to the left of it and the timber yards and saw mill which processed thousands of tons of imported wood each year. The bottom left hand corner of the photograph contains evidence of the old railway line. Near the centre of the picture is a piece of waste land which was later to become part of the Longhill Industrial Estate.

Down at the docks

Thirteen proud men pose with this railcar-mounted fire pump on a local railway siding. It was the early 1920s, and the pump, like most of its kind, was steam driven. It is quite possible that the picture was taken soon after the great fire in Hartlepool's Cleveland Road which occurred in 1922. An area covering almost 40 acres was affected and around 50 buildings were destroyed. This railcar-mounted water pump would have been the major weapon in the armoury of the fire fighters tasked with tackling any outbreak of fire. Their job would have been difficult, with only limited training in the art of tackling major blazes and little in the way of tools and equipment. Breathing apparatus was, of course, unheard of at the time. The dock areas were packed with inflammable material - including the Match Factory at Swainson Dock which caught fire and burned to the ground in 1954.

Above: The days when Hartlepool was a busy shipbuilding port are remembered here in this picture taken soon after the end of the Second World War. Once the biggest employer in the area, it is fitting that William Gray's shipyard has prominence in the scene. Gray's Shipyard is shown slightly to the left of centre here, with characteristic scaffolding surrounding a vessel under construction. The picture affords a good view of the docks and the houses and industrial areas closely wrapped around them, seemingly in defiance of the nearby North Sea. In the distance the Coal Dock, Jackson Dock, Central Dock and Union Dock can be seen. The changes which have taken place in the half-century or so since this scene was captured have been enormous, making the landscape here almost unrecognisable to anyone familiar with it at the time.

Below: The tranquillity of Victoria Dock is conveyed particularly well by this lovely photograph from 1965. The water looks smooth and inviting but the small vessels quietly moored here would be used to more dramatic and testing conditions when battling against the elements to make a living. This was the centre of Hartlepool's foothold in the deep sea fishing industry - undoubtedly one of the oldest as well as the most difficult commercial pursuits associated with the area. On the quayside there are several examples of the small companies which made their living from providing support for the fishing vessels and their owners. Among these are the *Hartlepool Marine Servicing Company* and *Griggs* the seine set manufacturers. A short distance away a massive ice producing factory could be found. Of course, there were dozens of other firms involved with repairing fishing vessels and all the equipment found on them, as well as all the clothing, storage, transportation and market facilities required by a busy fishing port.

Right: A tranquil dock scene dating from the 1960s and featuring the *Toki Arrow,* registered in Bergen.

By the time this picture was taken the writing was already on the wall for the future of Hartlepools' once thriving port activities. Soon shipments of coal and timber would be would down almost to a standstill. Glimmers of hope came in the form of new products such as pulp for paper production and the work associated with North Sea Gas and the nuclear power industry. Sadly these were not enough to maintain levels of employment at the port and a decade after this picture was taken saw trade reduced to almost nothing.

At first sight this looks like a scene from an under-ground coal mine, pit-props and air-powered tools being vital clues to the work being carried out. But no, these smiling men are working above ground, in the narrow space between the ground and the keel of a vessel under construction at Grays Shipyard. The men are riveters, responsible for the thousands of rivets holding the giant steel plates together on the S.S Ramso. The first large ship to have an iron hull was the S.S Great Britain, built in Bristol in 1843. At this time shipbuilding of any kind was still in its infancy in Hartlepool, but the availability of supplies of coal and later steel was to change all that within a relatively short time. By the outbreak of the First World War the output of steel ships had reached 150,000 tons per year. The Hartlepools prosperity was founded mainly upon success in the field of heavy industries. During wartime activities in this category, including shipbuilding, iron and steel production and coal mining traditionally do very well, but are vulnerable to the effects of cheap foreign imports and fluctuations in demand at other times.

Below: This picture dates from 1961 and features a group of students from the College of Art engrossed in their study of the Coal Dock and Staithes. The handling of cargoes of coal ceased in 1971, heralding a general period of near inactivity in the docks area during the 1970s. A young student can be seen sitting on the wall on the right and we are told that others were standing behind the photographer being instructed in the art of composition. Shipbuilding activity is taking place in the distance and the building on the right are the distinctive Dock Offices complete with ornate clock tower upon its roof. The large crane belonging to *Grays Central Marine Engineering Works* was a landmark in Hartlepool for decades. The young people in the picture were about to be thrown into the *swinging sixties* - probably the most dynamic decade of the twentieth century in terms of social values and attitudes. It was the era of the mini-skirt and the minicar, of cannabis, C.N.D and the Beatles. Changes were afoot in society which would change the lives of these young Hartlepool folk forever.

Right: A view of Jacksons Dock dating from 1968, some 116 years after it was created in 1852. Soon after the Jackson Dock was opened it was followed by the creation of the Timber Dock, the Timber Ponds and the Swainson Dock. At this time timber imports were still a large proportion of the trade handled by the port and a large stockpile of timber can be seen on the quayside in the foreground of the picture. The fortunes of the port as a timber importer relied, to a great extent, on the demand for wood in the coal mining industry (pit props), and house building and construction industries. The post-war domestic house building programme led to a large rise in demand for imported timber throughout the country and this helped keep the port busy during the period. Coal was another important element in the makeup of Hartlepools' port activity. Coal shipments ended in 1971 after a period of decline. This was virtually the final blow for the docks, making the 1970s one of the worst decades in the history of trade at the port.

Below: The sad sight of Victoria Terrace in the days shortly before the demolition men moved in to put the once proud properties out of their misery. The photograph was taken in March 1965 when parts of the terrace were still in use either for residential or retail purposes. The vandals had already begun smashing windows on the upper floors and vegetation can be seen sprouting from the guttering on the roof. The once-busy Victoria Cafe had closed for business and was showing signs of decay. Outside the cafe someone had just finished washing a light-coloured Austin A35 van. The popular light van was used by many small businesses and would have been a common sight around the town. On the left of the photograph the buffer-stops of the railway sidings are in view, reminding us of a time when this area was a thriving commercial centre and well-to-do residential district where sea captains and professional people lived.

Right: This inspiring photograph was taken for publicity purposes in March 1964. It features three smart police officers and their two keen Alsatian dogs on patrol in the docks. The backdrop for the picture is provided by four very sturdy cranes with massive lifting capacity designed to handle thousands of tons of cargo over a period of many decades. The proximity of the railway sidings and the goods wagon is a clue to the importance of the rail network to the success of the docks and Hartlepool's position as an active port. At the time this picture was taken all was not going well for the local economy. In the early part of the decade unemployment was running at around twice the national average. Gray's Shipyard was the last shipyard in Hartlepool and the region was devastated in 1962 when news of its closure was announced. The cause was said to be the decline in demand for smaller vessels (Grays were unable to produce the larger, more popular ships from their yard in Hartlepool), under investment and competition from subsidised foreign shipbuilders. To most families the cause didn't matter, for the closure of Grays meant long years of hardship and unemployment for many of them.

Shopping spree

Inset: Britain's favourite retailer, *Marks and Spencer,* arrived in Hartlepool very early in the development of the company. The firm's first presence in the area took the form of a market stall located in the busy market from 1894. They continued to trade at the market for a period of 18 years until 1912. The shop at 39 Lynn Street - pictured here - was opened in 1909, making a three year overlap with the market stall in the years shortly before the outbreak of the First World War. The shop at number 39 Lynn Street was successful in gaining a foothold in Hartlepool's shopping arena until the firm outgrew it in 1926. It was an interesting sales tactic to put the words 'Admission Free' on the sign above the shop window, giving the impression that the shop was so good that people might think of *paying* to enter it!

Below: After 17 years successful trading at 39 Lynn Street Marks and Spencer had outgrown the premises and needed to move on. Luckily they were able to relocate to the larger property situated at 47-49 Lynn Street and the new store opened on 20th August 1926. Even this larger store had to be extended twice in later years to cope with the growth of the business, such was the popularity of M&S with Hartlepool folk. The redevelopment of the central shopping area in the late 1960s brought with it compulsory purchase orders for properties along Lynn Street, including the store pictured here. It closed after over 43 years, on 28th October 1969.

Within two days the new store, with nearly three times the space and bright modern fittings of the old one, opened in the new Middleton Grange shopping centre.

Above: It is difficult to imagine what might have been going through the mind of this brown-overalled grocer as he poses for the photographer outside his busy shop. Gallons Ltd was situated on Lynn Street and did a roaring trade in all things edible. A great deal of time had been spent creating this magnificent window display which would have been irresistible to passing shoppers. Some of the signs in the window make interesting reading to the modern eye. Our favourite is 'Lovely Little Hams 3/6 each' - the thought of which is enough to make a vegetarian blow a fuse. Non-meat eaters could have filled up on tinned fruit, with peaches of *good* quality being available for 10 1/2d (about 4p) and those of *fancy* quality 11d per tin. The price of bacon was 11d per pound (just less than 5p) and eggs were on sale for 1/6 per dozen. It is likely that the picture dates from just before the outbreak of the Second World War, and within a few years the produce mentioned here was subject to strict rationing.

THE COUNTY BOROUGH OF WEST HARTLEPOOL.

ELECTRICITY DEPARTMENT

OFFERS
Electric
Light
Energy
Cookers
Toasters
Radiators
Installations
Curlers
Inclusive
Terms

Y

WATER HEATING BY ELECTRICITY
IS SAFETY WITH ECONOMY

Call at the Showrooms—

67, CHURCH STREET.

Telephone 2268.

HAMPTON E. BLACKISTON
BOROUGH ELECTRICAL ENGINEER

Above: The York Road premises of D. M Brown in West Hartlepool were set out with state-of-the -art equipment when this picture was taken. The scene is believed to date from the mid 1930s and the charming clock in the background tells us that it was recorded at 10.30 am. The business must have been successful, judging by the number of weighing scales, bacon slicers and assistants who were engaged at the shop. Some of the products on offer would be alien to some younger consumers of today. Pigs cheek might be one example. Other products on offer included potted meat, pork roll, bacon and ham. Hams can be seen hanging from the ceiling and a display of Libby's canned tomatoes adorned the shelves behind the pretty assistants. These were the days long before many goods were pre-packed, and shopping was as much a social activity as a chore. Life was organised at a slower pace than we are used to in modern times, and people seemed to have more time for a smile and a friendly word in the course of their day to day activities.

Above right: Some younger readers may find it hard to imagine the times when supplies of electricity and gas were provided by the local borough council in towns and cities throughout the land. From the earliest days of the availability of these facilities - which are now taken for granted - it was left to local boroughs to find the resources necessary to begin a reliable and safe service. Gas supplies were introduced first followed by electricity supplies which were first applied to electric lighting in public places. The availability of electricity made a big impact on industry. Small electric motors could be used in factories making the use of overhead lineshafts and large steam powered engines virtually redundant.

This advert relates to the County Borough of Hartlepool Electricity Department with showrooms based at 67 Church Street. Power had been generated in Hartlepool at the Burn Road facility since 1901. The North Eastern Electricity Board was established in later years and the whole industry was centralised when the *Central Electricity Generating Board* was set up in 1926.

It has been said that relatively few older buildings of exceptional architectural interest remain in Hartlepool, but an exception must surely be the imposing former Co-operative store. Situated on the corner of Stockton Street and Park Road, the grey portland stone monument to the co-operative retail movement no longer serves the shoppers of Hartlepool - which is a great pity. Thankfully the significance of the quality of the fine architecture has not escaped the powers-that-be who have designated the property a Grade II listed building. When the Hartlepool Co-operative Society opened the store in 1915 it dominated retailing in the area. The timing of the opening was not ideal of course, being one year into the First World War. Consciousness of the war was at a high level, not least because of the German bombardment of the Hartlepools from warships in December 1914. With 112 civilians and 9 military personnel killed, and many hundreds injured, the raid caused more human misery than all the World War II bombing attacks combined. Despite being created in difficult times the Co-op went on to be a household favourite in the district, drawing customers from miles around.

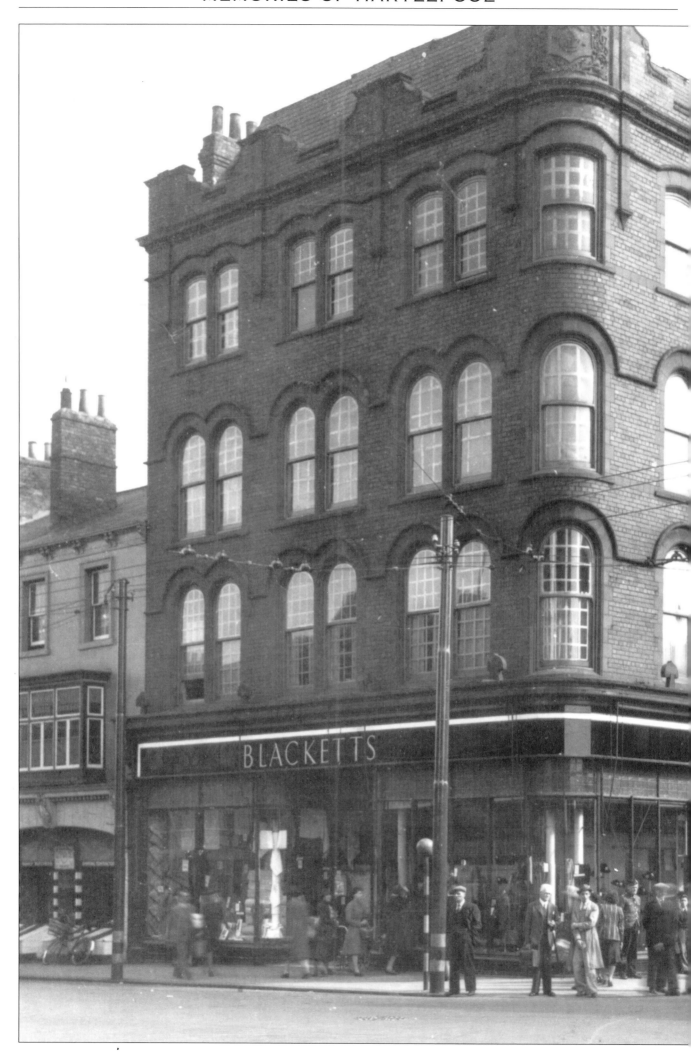

IN LATER YEARS THE ORNATE BRICKWORK AT ROOF LEVEL WAS SQUARED OFF TO GIVE THE BUILDING A MORE MODERN APPEARANCE

A late 1930s view of the Blacketts store which stood on the corner of Church Street and Whitby Street. In later years the ornate brickwork at roof level was squared off to give the building a more modern but less pleasing appearance. Overhead power cables are much in evidence along the busy street, providing power for the trolley buses which carried workers and shoppers from their homes into the town. Signs of wartime are a clue to the date of the photograph. The only motor vehicle in the scene is a light van on the right. It has a broad white outline painted around its mudguards and wings to provide a warning to others travelling in the blackout, the bottom of the poles holding up the power lines for the trolley network had received similar treatment. The upstairs windows of Blacketts had had white tape fixed to look like part of the window frames. This was, however, anti-blast tape, designed to restrict the phenomenon of flying glass in the event of a bomb falling nearby.

Above: This photograph shows the interior of Duncan's grocery shop on York Road as it appeared in 1966. The world of shopping has seen many changes throughout this century and these have been mirrored on the retail streets of Hartlepool as much as anywhere. The earliest form of shopping took place at open markets under the authority granted by the Crown or his regional representative. Markets were held on specific days to enable participants and their customers to travel together for security reasons as much as for the convenience it achieved. Shopping as we recognise it today can be traced back the Victorian era with fortunes being made by independent retailers and giants such as the Co-op alike. There have been many developments along the way - such as the introduction of weighing machines and cash registers, pre-packed (including canned) food and, much later, the age of self service shopping. In modern times the act of shopping is generally closely connected with our obsession with the motor car. This had led to the development of out-of-town shopping centres and giant retail parks - all of which threaten traditional shopping scenes such as this one.

Right: *Memories of Hartlepool* are bound to be rekindled by this nostalgic view, captured at the corner of Church Street and Tower Street. The photograph dates from October 1966 and the central feature of the shot is the business owned by Andrew C. Watt which sold the unusual combination of tobacco and toys. A sign in one window promotes Tri-ang, Dinky and Corgi models while Capstan cigarettes are promoted in the window around the corner. A variety of cars from the 1960s add character to the scene, including the delightful Riley saloon, a Bedford CA van complete with unusual sliding driver and passenger doors.

On the move

Below: A little girl can be seen looking out of the rear window of this single-decker trolley bus in 1927. The vehicle, registration number EF 2121, was about to set off on the Foggy Furze route over seven decades ago. Vehicles like this were introduced on the passenger routes of Hartlepool from February 1924. They were quieter and more comfortable than trams and within three years of the *trolley age* all the trams were taken out of service. The reign of the trolley bus lasted until 1953 when diesel driven motorbuses finally won the day. Each of the two *Hartlepools* provided its own motorbus service, with distinctive livery, from 1953 onwards.

Right: The launching ceremony for any ship, no matter how big or small, is an emotional and highly-charged experience, no matter how many times it has been witnessed. Shipbuilding was an important, if not vital aspect of economic life in the district when this picture was taken in 1960. The activity represented the area's biggest category of employment and skills in the industry had been learned and passed down through generations.

The photograph shows the launching of the *Mabel Warwick* at the Central Dock. Backs are turned to camera as the new vessel makes her first tentative movement away from her berth, shepherded by small diesel tugs positioned to keep her out of danger in her first minutes at sea. The journey would only be a short one, however, to the fitting-out berth where craftsmen would equip the *Mabel Warwick* for a life on the ocean wave.

E.F. 2121

'We sell Hercules on easy terms'... proclaimed a sign in Johns' window. Hercules was a make of cycle and the easy terms would have been attractive to anyone hoping to make the transition from 'bussing it' to work to a more independent form of transport. The proprietor of Johns Ltd was John Taylor and the gentleman himself can be seen standing in the shop doorway. The business was located along Stockton Road, close to St. Aidans, and supplied new cycles as well as all the bits and pieces necessary to keep them in roadworthy condition. The impressive fascia sign above the shop window informed potential customers that Johns Ltd were agents for Triumph, Hercules, New Hudson, Phillips, Norman and Armstrong machines. Some of these brands exist to this day but many have sadly fallen by the wayside. An interesting feature of the picture is the display of plastic capes hanging by the shop doorway. These transparent waterproof garments were light enough and small enough to be carried in the pocket or saddlebag of the cyclist concerned, and were a boon in unexpected wet weather. Like so many other businesses of this nature Johns went on to sell television and radio equipment in later years.

At work

PRODUCTION AT CEREBOS SALT FACTORY BEGAN IN 1906, THE RAW MATERIAL BEING SOURCED FROM LOCAL NATURAL BRINE WELLS

The hand-written caption on the back of this print describes it as being 'an evangelical meeting at the Cerebos Salt Factory in 1925.' It is far more likely that the scene depicts lunchtime in the Cerebos canteen, with a dozen or so 'evangelists' taking advantage of a captive audience of not-so-impressionable young ladies. If the expressions on the faces of the female workforce are anything to go by the presence of the evangelists was not universally welcomed. Salt production at this location began in 1906, the raw material being sourced from the natural brine wells. Saxa and Cerebos salt was packed and dispatched until production was transferred to Cheshire in 1970. Various other grocery products were made here over the years, including custard powder, jelly and blancmange.

Above: Less than a year after the outbreak of the Second War, in July 1940, the Tin Box Factory was severely damaged by an enemy air raid. This picture shows the aftermath of the raid on Thornton Street and Villiers Street.

The premises where the business owned and run by Cecil. M. Yuill was based can be seen in the distance, with a military officer striding past it in a determined manner.

Sturdy wooden barriers were intended to keep traffic and curious pedestrians away from the bomb site while workmen and company officials made the site safe and attempted to salvage any useable items from the wreckage. During the same raid the Temperance Hotel was completely destroyed by a direct hit.

Right: This very orderly industrial scene gives the impression of boom times ahead for Hartlepool's steel manufacturing industry. The picture was taken in the early 1960s and the plant featured on it was the South Works of the South Durham Steel and Iron Company Ltd. Work on the plant had begun in 1958 and took around three years to complete. It was linked to a sister plant known as the 'North Works' by a railway and produced steel plate and pipe. In 1967 the firm was the largest employer in Hartlepool with more than 5500 people engaged in steel production here. But decline set in and thousands of jobs were lost. Steel production ended at the North Works in 1971; within six years the site would be flattened and the closure of the South Works (with the exception of the Pipe Mill), announced to the alarm of local people.

WHETHER

Your New Home

is to be a HOUSE *or a* BUNGALOW

have it DESIGNED *and* ERECTED *by*

*Finance
arranged
if desired*

*Well built
Labour Saving
and
Moderate
in Cost.
Erected in
any District.*

Harland & Parker,
SPRING GARDEN ESTATE
West Hartlepool.

And
CHAPEL ROAD,
BILLINGHAM.
Telephone Norton 329

Left: This advertisement dates from around 1930 and features a pair of semi-detached houses that most of us would love to own. They were obviously new when the advertisement was published, making them around 70 years old at the time of writing. The houses were spacious and well-equipped when built with 'modern' kitchens and bathrooms, all features which we take for granted these days, but in the 1930s (and much later in many cases) inside toilets, bathrooms and hot running water were things that could only be dreamed of by some householders. From the late 1920s onwards there was a determined effort to upgrade the housing stock in the district on the part of the two *Hartlepools*. The depression hit 1920s and 30s made the task a difficult one with local heavy industry being badly hit, inevitably causing high unemployment. Like so many industrial towns the quality of much of the area's housing stock left much to be desired, with thousands of houses being unfit for human habitation. New housing estates were built at Raby Road and Rift House in the 1920s; The West View housing estate in the 1930s, as well as the Fens and Seaton Carew in later years. There was controversy when the Croft was demolished in 1938 and again when Sandwell Chare was covered over during the same year.

Far left: An abundant supply of crystal clear spring water was one of the main reasons for the establishment of the Lion Brewery in the heart of the village of Stranton around a century and a half ago. The small business grew to become a major player in the regional brewing industry which slaked the thirst of generations of steel workers and shipbuilders in the north east. The brewery was established by William Waldon in 1852, then developed by his widow and son after his untimely death in 1854.

Around a decade or so later John Cameron became involved in the business, taking over completely in 1872. Over a period of time the company bought out smaller brewing businesses throughout the district and Cameron himself rose to fame as a successful entrepreneur and philanthropist. This photograph shows the simple but dignified exterior of the Stockton Street brewery as it appeared in 1967.

Above: The 'Northern Gas Making Plant' under construction at Hartlepool is pictured as it appeared in January 1964. Any glimmer of good news and hope for the future was eagerly grasped when the photograph was taken, for the *Hartlepools* were going through a torrid time in the early 1960s. The closure of the last shipyard in the area two years earlier had made the district a regional unemployment blackspot. The discovery of North Sea gas and oil brought hope to local industrialists and those concerned with the economic prospects of the town. With more than one in ten workers on the dole and no sign of either a local or national improvement, concerns began to rise. By October Harold Wilson was elected with the first Labour Government for 13 years.

Right: This small brass foundry was owned by J.J. Hardy and Sons Ltd and operated from these premises at the corner of Old Cemetery Road. The scene was recorded in November 1967, so the *Ford Corsair* on the right would have been a couple of years old by that time. It is interesting to look back and remember how small industrial workshops used to look in the era depicted here. Of course, many small, light industrial companies still work from premises like these, but purpose-built industrial units on out of town estates are now more typical. Back in 1967 the thoughts of local people would have been focused on the extensive demolition of the central area of the Borough of Hartlepool and the imminent construction of the Middleton Grange Shopping Centre.

A family concern in metal forming

J.J. Hardy & Sons is a company with a long history firmly rooted on Teesside. Founded in 1856 as brass founders and engineers, the company has remained a family concern to the present day, though the family concerned has changed.

The year 1856 was a propitious time for such a company to be born. It was almost 30 years since the very first passenger train had run from Darlington to Stockton. The industrial revolution was in full swing. A vast iron and steel industry was springing up on Teesside to supply the busy shipyards with raw materials. Engine builders to power the ships, were establishing new factories.

A steady demand for non ferrous castings for use both as bearings and for pressure tight valve castings, was swiftly growing.

Above: W.H Hardy Stood outside 11 Church Stret, West Hartlepool around 1903..
Below: "Photograph courtesy of Mrs. E. Harvey whose Great Grandfather, Thomas Robson Harrison, is second from the right, back row".

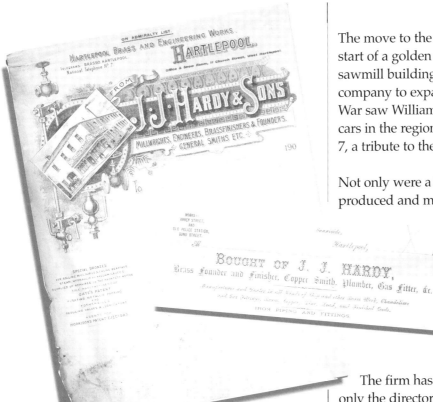

The move to the Throston Bridge brass works was the start of a golden era for the company and the ex-sawmill building proved an ideal base for the company to expand. The era before the First World War saw William Henry Hardy, with one of the first cars in the region and the National Telephone Number 7, a tribute to the firm's early involvement in IT.

Not only were a huge volume of brass castings being produced and machined at this time, but the company were manufacturing pressure gauges, carrying out black-smith work and even developed an early petrol engine for installation in small boats. A retail operation was also established in West Hartlepool.

The firm has always been loyally served by not only the directors but also by the staff. A good example of loyalty and dedication was provided by Tot Walker. He joined the company in 1904 as a boy of

The firm was set up in Abbey Street in East Hartlepool and the Old Police Station, Bond Street. From its inception it was associated with Hartlepool's shipbuilding industry. The small firm supplied the local iron and steel works with their requirements for such castings as rolling mill brasses, bearings and bushes. In the 1880's a move from here was made to Throston Bridge where the company remained until 1968.

John James Hardy had a large family though as was the unfortunate expectation at the time many of them died. William Hardy, born in 1855, carried on the firm after the death of John James in 1903.

fourteen. After serving an apprenticeship in the tool room he was appointed works manager and served the company continuously until his retirement in 1960. He was known and respected throughout the North East as a man of integrity and a fine engineer. At various times his sons, a nephew, and his half-brother George, also worked for the company.

Top Left: Unique, early letterheads The first addressed at Throston Bridge and the second from Sunniside, Hartlepool from 1870. Centre: Brass Shop, first floor J.J.Hardy - before 1900. Left: Laura Nutley, core making late 19th century, latterly maid in William Henry's household."

The company survived the difficulties of the economic depression that followed the First World War. In 1938 William H. Hardy, now aged 83, decided to sell the controlling interest in his family business and chose the well-known Hartlepool entrepreneur Cllr. T.H. Pailor (known as Tommy) to be the new owner.

1938 was a memorable year for Tommy Pailor, because as well as purchasing a fine old family business, he got married to Marion Temperley.

For the next 25 years the front office at JJH became Tommy Pailor's nerve centre from which he ran a complex business empire - the companies included two iron foundries, a steel fabrication business, not to mention foreign trade, land development, a doll factory, and the building of cinemas. Between times sitting as an Independent Councillor for the St. Hilda Ward. Tommy was mayor of the old Borough of Hartlepool for four years 1941-44, and he continued to run J.J. Hardy's as a profitable and successful business until his sudden death in 1963.

He always considered that his finest achievement was when, as Chairman of the Hartlepool War Weapons Week Committee in May1941 they aimed to raise £75,000. The Committee achieved the total of £309,000.

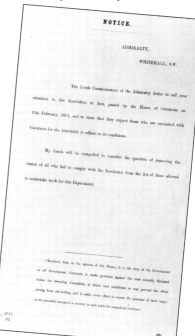

Top: An early view of J.J Hardy, Brassworks. **Left and right:** *Pages of admiralty list in 1904.* **Above:** *T.H. Pailor, Chairman and Managing Director 1938 - 1963.*

Thomas Temperley Pailor (known as Tom) joined the business in 1956 and under the tutelage of Higham Lancaster in the foundry and George Walker in the machine shop served an interesting and varied apprenticeship.

The sudden death of Tommy Pailor in 1963 saw the start of an era of great change because not only J.J. Hardy's but the town of Hartlepool and surrounding area were about to see more changes than had occurred in the previous century.

In the early 1960's shipbuilding ceased in the town and was followed by a slow decline in the manufacture of steam turbines and large marine diesel engines. Such companies as Richardsons Westgarth, William Gray's, Durham Paper Mills, closed down. The South Durham Steel & Iron Co., however, continued to prosper and constructed a new integrated steel works on the site of the old Greatham Airport.

Tom Pailor was appointed Works Director on the death of his father and remembers the time :

"On becoming a Director in 1963 I soon realised the companies strengths - a loyal skilled workforce, good client base, excellent reputation and low cost manufacturing base - were not going to be enough

to survive in the turbulent economic years of the late 60's and early 1970's.

In 1963 both the foundry and machine shop needed new plant and processes. The principal difficulties to overcome were limited financial resources, traditional three storey building with wooden floors, the vast cellar caused problems with machine foundations, but most importantly the lack of three phase electricity, making the purchase of modern machine tools virtually impossible.

By 1967, encouraged by the then Board of Marion Pailor and Alex Brown, we had installed oil fired smelting, CO_2 core making and a number of second hand modern machine tools. This plant increased production dramatically and was found to be easily re-installed at our new factory in Brenda Road.

What today's factory inspectorate would have made of our fine old building at Throston Bridge and our Heath Robinson activities I shudder to think.

1967 was a momentous year in the history of the company. It started well with the birth of Andrew T. Pailor, but the death of Managing Director, Marion Pailor, in September was followed by a compulsory purchase order from the old Hartlepool Borough Council who, in their last few months before amalgamation, decided they needed our fine old building to create another open space."

Top: *An old shaper in the foreground and in the background a modern Alba shaper. George (Jossy) Walker, Tom's tutor and mentor butts half brasses. Dated 1968.* *Above:* *The brass Shop in 1968 shows how little things have changed since the Page two picture.* *Left:* *Foreman moulder Dick Wilkinson supervises the pouring of bronze, assisted by Higham Lancaster and another moulder in 1950s.*

The Directors considered many options before locating their new home at Brenda Road, Hartlepool, adjacent to the newly built South Durham Steel & Iron works. The factory was built by C.M. Yuill's, to a design by Ian Nelson. It was of a semi detached layout with the foundry and machine shop operations now separated and services and facilities all located in a convenient manner.

The company deposited at the foundation laying ceremony, a record of both its old and new activities, together with a set of the coinage of the day. The move to the new factory caused the business to focus more

on the machining of parts than on the casting, although both activities continued to prosper. During the 1970's however the steel industry on Teesside began to decline and steel production and rolling in Hartlepool finally ceased. The demand for castings throughout the UK declined dramatically and it was soon apparent to the Board that further rationalisation would be necessary.

In 1974 the company purchased the foundry operations of Middlesbrough's long established brass foundry, John Livingston, from Tom's lifelong friend, Bernard Ord. It was Bernard who had supplied the first secondhand machine tools that were installed at Throston Bridge and his company - NMT Ltd. - has continued to supply machine tools to the firm up to the present day.

The foundry operations were now transferred to the Middlesbrough foundry of John Livingston and continues there to this day under the control of George Barnett. The merger of the Hardy foundry with

Livingston's meant the combination of 200 years' experience in non-ferrous sand cast production.

The newly vacated foundry building in Brenda Road was converted into a medium machine shop with slightly heavier machine tools and a further heavy machine shop was constructed on the Brenda Road site with a lifting capacity of 20 tons. Very large vertical and horizontal borers, together with a 26ft planing machine, were installed. This diversification enabled the company to spread its machine shop activities over a broader spectrum of clients.

A basic and far reaching change now occurred in engineering technology and J.J. Hardy's was once again right at the front in this ever changing world. For thousands of years metal had been formed by melting and

pouring into moulds, usually made from sand.

The electronic revolution which started with the first computers, subsequently made this method of

manufacture less popular for metal items of the highest integrity. Computer Numerically Controlled machine tools began to appear in the mid 1970's, taking over from the rather primitive numerically controlled machine tools, which were introduced in the late 1960's.

CNC machine tools made it possible for computers to carve from solid metal, high integrity metal components with extremely tight tolerances and surface finish. Tom Pailor had followed the development of this technology since the late 60's and in 1976 the company purchased one of the first CNC machine tools installed in the North East and in so doing unleashed a new revolution at J.J. Hardy's. This development was greeted with some scepticism and trade union reaction was initially unfavourable, but by 1981 the company had become totally committed to this new form of manufacture, and by 1998 was to have installed 14 such machine tools.

Above Left: Laying the foundations on the 2nd October 1968, pictured is Madge and Tom Pailor.
Right: Heavy machine shop under construction, with column for 26ft planer about to be installed 1975.
Below Left: John Popplewell and Jimmy Johnson - Foundry in Middlesbrough 1990s Aluminium gearcase for London Underground.

1981 saw the retirement of Alex Brown. He had joined the company on its purchase by the Pailor family and served the firm loyally as Company Secretary until his retirement. His service being only broken by the war years, when he flew Spitfires with great distinction in the Royal Air Force.

Following in the Hardy tradition of commitment and service, Alex recruited a young graduate, Graham Clyburn, in 1975 whom he trained to take over on his retirement. Graham was subsequently appointed a Director of the business and has been responsible for the installation of the latest computerised accountancy software and an excellent financial control system, so vital in today's marketplace.

The company continued in the 1980's to serve both its traditional steel and foundry clients, but also manufactured many parts for the mining industry and the booming North Sea Oil area.

Madge Pailor was recruited through marriage in 1962 and was appointed Company Secretary in 1981. Her secretarial skills were very useful in handling the new type of challenges that a CNC business brings.

During the 1980's the company installed further additional CNC equipment and continued to see a decline in its traditional business areas.

A good illustration of the flexibility of the CNC machine tools was a contract undertaken at this time for the local Brewery, Camerons, when over 5000 bar countermounts were machined from brass bar and tube by our CNC machine tools and soon became recognised throughout the UK for their outstanding looks.

In 1984 Tom's son Andrew, joined the business working for companies throughout the UK and also spending time at J.J Hardy's studying the programming and setting of CNC machine tools. Andrew has travelled worldwide identifying the very best processes for CNC machining.

Quality has always been a trade mark of the company and in 1989 the Directors decided to apply for BS 5750 part 2 (now replaced by ISO 9002). The picture on page 3 of the company's Admiralty List Approval shows the company's tradition in this respect and the existing systems prove a successful basis for the company's accreditation on 1st January 1990. This proved an excellent harbinger for the last decade of the millennium.

Parts manufactured by Hardy's CNC machine tools are to be found on some of the deepest subsea well heads, at the bottom of the deepest mine in Europe, on construction sites worldwide, and nearly every motorway carries

vehicles with Hardy's axle components. Readers travelling by rail will find that most journeys on the UK rail network will be on rolling stock carrying "Hardy" parts.

Top: Butler Elgamill installed 1984. ***Above:*** *BS5750 Certificate next to brewery countermount.* ***Left:*** *The 12-tool turret on the Hitachi Seiki lathe from 1979.*

The company has always had a great tradition of training apprentices and to mark the launch of a Modern Apprenticeship programme, which we pioneered in Hartlepool, a Skills Reunion Day was held. The oldest surviving Hardy trained apprentices visited the works and met with current employees, and in particular the first three Modern Apprentices.

During the reunion the company announced a new training initiative. In conjunction with the Tees Valley TEC the firm offered two "Modern Apprenticeships" for each of the following five years. This was a conscious step to ensuring the firm's viability in the 21st Century. A curriculum was drawn up, embracing both on and off the job training to provide a balanced apprenticeship in which traditional craft skills of turning, milling and fitting would be learned, together with a mixture of high tech activities in the information technology field.

Left: J.J. Hardy reunion in 1994.
Below: Three Modern Apprentices with MP for Hartlepool Peter Mandelson .

The late 1990's have seen further innovative and exciting investment decisions by the firm. One of our first CNC machine tools was purchased from Hitachi Seiki (UK) and this business relationship has prospered since the mid 1970's.

Two examples have been the installation of a HiCell in 1994. This type of machine is now used by nearly every major Grand Prix motor racing team for the one-hit production of complex parts and made its first appearance in the UK at Hardy's.

The installation in 1998 of a Hitachi CS20 was again a pioneering decision. This automatic loading vertical lathe has tremendously high production rates, allied to extreme accuracy.

Hardy's realise that maintaining high standards is not a matter of chance. Their stated quality policy is that "the best way to assure quality is by working in a systematic fashion to documented procedures". All company employees have responsibility for this.

In 1998 Andrew Pailor became Managing Director. He is the third member of the Pailor family to serve a craft apprenticeship to the trade in which they specialise.

The company's success and survival over so many years would not have been possible without the commitment and effort from all its employees. The directors are the first to recognise this and wish to make this article a testimony to their achievement.

Only two families have run this firm. The help and co-operation of the Hardy family in the preparation of this article is a confirmation of the affection in which they still hold the business, which bears their family name.

The company would record its appreciation to the following:

Minnie Boyle (nee Baines)
is Great Grand Daughter of the Founder.
Queenie Griffiths.
Peter Hogg.
The late Robert Wood.
Mrs. E. Harvey.
Hartlepool Reference Library & Museum.

Above: From left to right Madge Pailor, Company Secretary, Tom Pailor, Chairman, Andrew Pailor, Managing Director, and Graham Clyburn, Commercial Director, from old tools to modern tools.
Left: The new Hitachi CS20.

The company that created the Angel of the North

The Hartlepool Erection Company is one of Teesside's largest privately owned engineering companies. It commenced its operation in 1960 when Leonard Stalley, a constructional engineer for Clarence erection Company and Thomas Barron, a structural engineer for south durham Iron and Steel (later to be known as the British Steel Corporation) became partners in their own concern, doing site erection work of all types.

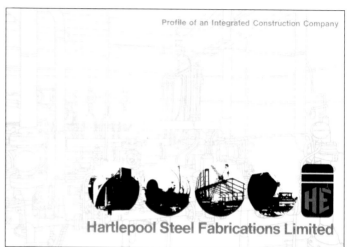

Profile of an Integrated Construction Company

Hartlepool Steel Fabrications Limited

For a time, since no 'works' were required but just a base where telephoned orders could be received, the firm's headquarters were at 209 Park Road, Mr Stalley's home. What was being offered for sale was the labour of the two partners and later that of their staff, together with the use of their erection equipment.

In 1963 the new company was doing sufficiently well to be able to take premises at the Graythorp Industrial Estate on the north side of the Tees.

Hartlepool Steel Fabrications Ltd was incorporated in 1966 to provide the manufacturing support to the already successful site erection business. Together, the companies

specialised in construction for the petrochemical, steel and allied industries. Over the years, the facilities were expanded to cover all possible requirements of those industries as far as structures, piping vessels, tanks and mechanical plant were concerned. The buildings consisted of a Pipe department with a surrounding stockyard, a Fabrication Shop and a covered extension intended for a future heavy Fabrication Shop.

Top: A cover of a 1970s brochure .
Left: Leonard Stalley one of the founders of the company.
Bottom: Typical small bore installation involving the company's fabrication and erection facilities.

The company undertook the complete design, detailing and fabrication of process plant pipework, pressure vessels and storage tanks from the enquiry stage to contract completion. The size of any structure made in the fabrication department was limited only by the department of the environment regulations. steel sections in thicknesses up to four inches and fabrications up to 40 tons in unit weight could be handled. Orders were taken for access platforms for oil rig deck modules, petro-chemical plants and associated industries. Most of these were erected on site by the company's own staff.

A specific erection service was offered, tailored to meet the customers' requirements. The highly skilled staff used mobile cranes up to 45 tons capacity and a comprehensive range of mobile welding plant, compressors and other site equipment. Work at this period included an up-shot heater for the Das-

Island project, weighing 63 tonnes and a hose rig structure for an oil terminal that was erected on the jetty area of the River Tees.

Above: A Fabricated Quench Tank leaving the company's Graythorpe premises en-route to site. The picture dates from the late 1970s.
Below: Modern-day assembly of a test vessel on site. The vessel is 55 metres long, 4.5 metres in diameter and 46mm thick.

A structure to support an oil rig Ballast tank each of its two sections weighing 18 tonnes was completed in seven days from receipt of order.

Pipework contracting followed in 1967 and from this time the Group has maintained a steady growth through the confidence of locally based customers who have increased their contract enquiries in line with the company's development and expansion.

The advent of off-shore rig building in the seventies presented the Group with an opportunity to extend its manufacturing skills for contracts which involved heavy engineering in the secondary support steelwork required in the building of off-shore platforms. It was also

Above: The interior of the workshop with work in progress on stair-towers for an offshore client.
Left: Modular Bridges, fabricated and assembled at the Graythorpe works and erected on site.
Facing page, top: The company's premises.
Facing page, bottom: An aerial view of the works with the completed 'Angel of the North' in the yard, awaiting transportation to its home.

platforms through to major plant structures including the process pipework. Site-based maintenance and general repair to existing plant has been part of the deal.

When the Tioxide Works at Greatham extended its production to include the new ICON plant, it awarded to the Hartlepool Erection Group the fabrication and erection of two main plant structures

involved with the concrete platform recently built at the Laing Offshore Yard.

Work has been secured from most of Britain's major companies. ICI on Teesside has awarded the company varied contracts from small access

and a storage building comprising some 550 tonnes of structural steelwork. HEG was also the main steelwork contractor for Cornings Ltd (Pyrex) of Sunderland when they extended their plant with the installation of a new melting furnace

BS 5750 for a considerable period of time and registration was approved in September 1991.

The Hartlepool Erection Group's success is based on flexibility combined with personal service, with each Company free to work individually or as part of a Group team.

The Group currently consists of:-
Hartlepool Erection Company Limited (1960)
This company provides a variety of erection and site services to the construction industry, including maintenance of existing plants and equipment and labour to suit clients' requirements. The company operates its own crane fleet up to 45 tonnes capacity and general site equipment such as weld sets, compressors, accommodation units and lockable stores.

Hartlepool Steel Fabrication Ltd (1966)
This company provides the manufacturing back up for HEG Ltd. It makes structural steelwork, tanks, vessels, modules, access platforms, ladders, ducting and platework from the basic supply services to the petro-chemical, offshore, gas and steel industries.

HEG works for British Gas, mainly on regulator and jet booster stations, installed throughout the North East and North West. Contracts include the fabrication and erection of pipework and impulse pipework which is a speciality of this company.

The list of clients is extensive and includes companies of all sizes. The very small as well as the very large are offered the same commitment to cost-effective engineering.

Quality assurance is of paramount importance. The company operated a management system to

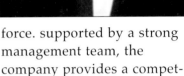

force. supported by a strong management team, the company provides a competitive, prompt and safe service.

Hartlepool Pipework Services Ltd (1988)
This company was comparatively recently formed to make a separate unit of the mechanical engineering services. it undertakes the supply and installation of all types of process plant pipework. It supplies skid units and modules to the petrochemical and gas industries.

Cleveland Dismantling Services Ltd (1988)
This company services all types of demolition and dismantling requirements, including licensed asbestos removal. Its industrial dismantling contracts are mostly with the chemical and steel industries throughout the north east and north west. It operates a fleet of specialised plant together with an experienced and skilled labour

To the industries it serves, the Group means the availability of a highly skilled , specialised and dependable service, but to the man - or woman - in the Hartlepool street, HEG is the company that supplied and erected the Angel of the North.

Above left: The Angel being lifted into place at its site next to the A1 at Low Fell, Gateshead.
Above right: Bill Stalley current managing director.
Below: The sight that greets most drivers as they enter the north.
Facing page, top: The construction of the Angel.
Facing page, bottom: The sheer size of the Angel is evident in this picture as it is transported to its home.

A history of building and designing houses

The Yuill Group of Companies was founded in 1926 by Cecil Mortley Yuill who was then 19 years old. After receiving training from his grandfather, a master plasterer, he became a bricklayer in a jobbing partnership with him, earning six shillings a week. He supplemented his income by playing a trumpet in a Hartlepool dance band for three nights each week, often playing until midnight before starting work the next morning at 4am. The savings his two jobs enabled him to make gave him the capital to start up his own building business.

In the years leading up to the Second World War, Cecil Yuill expanded his business, building houses in both the private and public sectors in his home town of Hartlepool. Being a small builder in the 1920s was not an easy task but, by 1932, Mr Yuill was building his first houses in Marlborough Street, Hartlepool. His first contract for 150 council houses came five years later.

Under pressure from the War Office, he became a Limited Company (Cecil M Yuill Ltd) in 1940. During the war he worked each Monday to Thursday repairing bomb damage for the London Borough of Wandsworth, together with the volunteer squad he had recruited. Each Friday to Sunday he spent building fortifications for the Admiralty in the North East.

After the war, the Company grew to become one of the North East's principal housing companies. In 1945 the turnover was £43,868. By 1952 it had risen to £321,000, principally from contract work. Within three years, that turnover had doubled and Cecil Yuill's strategic guidance saw the company acquire significant land purchases in the fifties and sixties. This meant the Company focused its attention and achieved its biggest success building private houses for the North East home purchaser, the first ones going up in Kingsley Avenue

By 1960 the turnover reached almost £800,000. Significant achievements were the building of Brierton Modern School, costing £350,000, the construction of 500 Unity houses and, most prestigious of all, the building of 208 three storey flats in Sunderland.

By 1968 a 64,000 square feet modern factory employed 120 operatives whilst the company also had 180 staff members and 1,150 workers on its 15 sites.

In 1969, after 43 years in business, the Company moved into purpose-built headquarters at Loyalty Road in Hartlepool, where it has remained ever since.

After Cecil Yuill's retirement in 1972, the Company was grateful to retain his services as a consultant. The business continued its growth to become one of the largest providers of private homes in the North East. In 1995, after seven decades of quality building for the local community,

over one fifth of all homes in Hartlepool and almost 30,000 homes throughout the North East are the product of the Yuill Group.

Throston and G R Howe were acquired in 1973 to add building services to the company's established reputation for building expertise.

It was a just reward when, in 1989 Yuill won the building industry's highest accolade - the National Housing Design Award - for an outstanding development at Collingwood Court, Morpeth, Northumberland.

Top: The T.T.T. film crew at West Park in spring 1969 with Mr Ron Norman. Above: Spread from Yuill's booklet in spring 1966. Left: Mr H Raine, Batch assembly foreman, with youngsters in the 1960's. Facing page top: Cecil M Yuill, Circa 1960's. Facing page bottom: Craftsmanship, Circa 1929.

The Group is still in private ownership and the current Chairman is Phillip Yuill, a son of the founder.

The Group is a building and property group based in Hartlepool, and operates in the North East, Yorkshire and East Midlands.

The house building division trades as Yuill Homes. It is a developer of high quality, traditionally built private housing, with a long established reputation in its North East territory. Its product range includes three and four bedroomed family homes through to five bedroomed executive properties, luxury apartments and town houses.

The design of the houses and the site and street layouts are produced by an experienced team of in-house architects and designers, often supplemented by nationally renowned architects resulting in a set of house ranges with distinctive designs and styles which are unique to the Yuill name.

The Company sells its product on each development, using its own highly-trained and experienced sales negotiators and makes full use of

Above: Yuill's first head office which had been head office for over 30 years.
Below: The Yuill factory in Brenda Road Hartlepool, the headquarters of Yuill Component Services in the sixties.

damaged houses with Cecil Yuill himself stayed with the firm until he finally stepped down in 1994. One of the members of the non-executive board was recruited by Mr Yuill 42 years ago as a trainee accountant. He was allowed to attend college on the basis that if he passed his examinations his fees would be refunded. Before retiring he went on to become Chief Executive of the Company. At least five of the Site Management team were Yuill apprentices who have been developed into their current role.

Although leading the field in new technologies and innovative thinking, the Group never forgets its foundations. Cecil Yuill once remarked that the people of the North East had been good to Yuills and that Yuills should never forget to be good to the people. The promise has been taken to heart by the Company. The Group moves into the 21st century with confidence - for itself and for the region which is its home.

Above: Inside the factory at Brenda Road Hartlepool where components were manufactured, circa 1960s.
Left: The Heritage range of homes from Yuill being advertised on a classic truck in front of one of their developments in 1991.
Bottom: An example of one of Yuill's houses showing progress in modern times.

branded sales and showhouse areas to enhance and display the product.

Even the most brilliant management needs a committed workforce in order to succeed.

Yuill workers are valued and well treated and repay with long service. A company bricklayer who served his time during the war repairing bomb-

Out of Africa

Sillars Construction was founded by Derek Sillars T.D when, following earlier experience in the construction industry and serving with the Royal Artillery during the war, he emigrated with his family to Cape Town South Africa and, after a short spell with a civil engineering company, formed Sillars Construction (P.T.Y.) Limited in 1951. The company grew and was to specialise in general road construction and asphalting as well as bridge building and the construction of railway sidings for industry.

The company prospered and expanded, even completing a major contract in Walvis Bay in what was then German South West Africa, now Namibia. It experienced impressive growth until the early sixties when increasing racial tension severely effected normal life in South Africa. Business prosperity became uncertain in what had then become a Republic and so the regrettable decision to sell up and return to the United Kingdom was taken by the family.

On return to the United Kingdom and, after a short spell as Regional Director for a major national company, Derek Sillars struck out on his own again forming Sillars Road Construction Limited on the 5th May 1965, after acquiring office and depot premises at Graythorp Industrial Estate, Hartlepool. His other founding Director was Frank Howitt, who had been the Surfacing Manager for Tarmac Roadstone in the North East.

From small beginnings and with a very dedicated workforce, the company began to grow and flourish, carrying out mainly road construction and re-surfacing work for Local Authorities, major industry, including the old nationalised industries, as well as private and

commercial sector work. In 1967 Tim Sillars joined the management team as the company continued to expand and a considerable amount of plant and machinery was gradually acquired as the company grew. In 1970, the company took a major step forward by the acquisition of Edwin Clarksons, a long established company in the same field, based at East Boldon near Sunderland. The take over of Clarksons, retaining all of its employees and with Roland Clarkson joining the board, almost doubled the size of the company overnight and gave it a considerable profile throughout the North East region. It was a very satisfactory move because the companies fitted so well together and with a very good team spirit many of the companies employees have served right through to retirement - for well over thirty years in many cases.

Sillars Road Construction Limited continued to grow and flourish, always maintaining a highly skilled and well-motivated workforce, supervised by competent

Above: The Lansdowne Yard in Cape Town. An asphalt mixer on mobile platform in 1956.
Left: Sillars Graythorp office surrounded by plant vehicles in 1966.

In 1980 Roland Clarkson sadly died and, in the re-organisation that followed, it was felt that the Company should separate its Road Construction and Civil Engineering operations. In 1981 Sillars formed the construction group Sillars Holdings Limited, chaired by Derek Sillars, with two operating construction subsidiaries - Sillars Road Construction Limited, the old company and Sillars (B&CE) Limited, the newly formed civil engineering arm of the group. The Sillars brothers, Tim, Tony and Duncan are on the board of each company.

management. It built up and maintained a wide range of plant and machinery ensuring that all projects are completed to the high standards that are maintained by the company.

Between 1970 and 1988, gradual further expansion took place and progress was consistently satisfactory, with the company beginning to take on more major civil engineering and drainage works as well as the more traditional road construction operations. To cope with this further expansion and, following the death of Frank Howitt, two further Sillars joined the Road Construction company in the late 1970's. Firstly, Duncan joined the construction management team to be followed shortly by Tony who became Company Secretary.

Sillars Road Construction Limited with Chairman Tim Sillars and Construction Director David Bell was to continue in it's traditional market of road construction, re-surfacing and repairs in the private, industrial and commercial market. This remains the situation today with the company undertaking a substantial amount of work from Local Authorities and heavy industry. It is involved with nearly all the major building and civil engineering companies in the North East. From the early eighties to mid-nineties the company had a long association of involvement with Cleveland County Council in the construction and resurfacing of the Clairville stadium cycle-track in Middlesbrough and the company annually sponsored the Cleveland Grand Prix for the "SILLARS TROPHY". Perhaps the most prestigious and noteworthy contract undertaken was the surfacing of the Nissan Test Track for the main Contractors Sir Robert McAlpine with a value of £800.000.

In terms of recent innovation, the company has introduced the Jet Repair System for the cost effective repairs of depressions and potholes in all types of surfaces including concrete. The

Above left: Derek Sillars and his wife Patricia opening first extension in 1971.
Above right: An aerial view of Clairville stadium, Middlesbrough.
Left: The newly formed Sillars Holdings Limited board of 1981.

equipment and machinery the company has completed major civil engineering projects throughout the North East region.

In the late 1980's the company increased it's expertise into the microtunnelling field, when it became the first civil engineering company in the region to purchase a microtunnelling machine. The company attracted much local and national publicity when it installed a 1.4Km pipeline under Yarm Road, Eaglescliffe as part of the sewer renovation contract. Pipe installation by this method meant that the road surface itself remained virtually undisturbed and disruption to traffic and pedestrians was therefore minimal. The tunnel Sillars bored was 28 meters longer than the previous world record held by a company in the South of England.

whole process is saving time and cost in the maintenance market and is proving to be a useful tool in the company's armoury. The company is quality assured under British Standard EN ISO 9002.

Sillars (B&CE) Limited, with chairman Duncan Sillars and Construction Director Stuart Mellis, was formed to undertake heavy civil engineering, including roads and sewer installations and to undertake new building alterations and improvement works for commercial and industrial developments in both the public and private sectors. This has continued to do very successfully - with very well qualified staff and it's own heavy

Above left: Tunneling through, picture showing part of microtunnelling machine. *Above right:* Trunk river main water crossing at Warkworth, Northumberland. *Below:* Gordon Wake being presented with a gold watch by Tim Sillars in 1991 after twenty five years service .

More recently, it has extended it's expertise into the field of trenchless technology by the purchase in early 1997 of Directional Drilling equipment. Currently the company is therefore able to offer a very wide experience in the heavy civil engineering field and in the installation of major sewerage and drainage schemes the company is particularly proud of the regeneration work completed at Manor Quay Sunderland, which received a Civic Trust Award. The company is a full member of the C.E.A. (Civil Engineering Association and Northern Limited) and the I.S.T.T. (International Society for Trenchless Technology).

In 1983 Derek Sillars became Non-Executive Chairman of Sillars Holdings Limited and, in the late 1980's the company started to develop a small business in the financial services field. The Sillars financial management business proved to be a successful "add-on" to the family business and Tony Sillars was to become Chairman of the company, S.F.M. (UK) Limited. Although outside the Construction Group, the company has a strong family link on the board and now, to realise it's full potential, the company is based at it's new office in Blackwell Lane, Darlington. It is expected that this move will enable considerable expansion to take place and so consolidate its position in the financial services market.

On the 9th August 1993 Derek Sillars announced his decision to retire and it was decided that his position as Non-Executive Chairman of Sillars Holdings Limited would be filled by Michael Sillars, who is a locally based Senior Partner of a national firm of Chartered Accountants.

Throughout the 1990's, in what has been in many ways a difficult time for the construction industry the group has continued to grow and flourish with tight control and sensible expansion. In 1998 group turnover is expected to well exceed £9,000,000 and yet it still remains essentially a friendly family business with a very loyal staff of some 120 people based at the Head Office at Hartlepool, together with it's regional offices at Jarrow and Sunderland. The Group has always maintained a keen interest in the welfare of it's workforce. It's Safety & Training programme is constantly reviewed and updated. Sillars keeps in close contact with the C.I.T.B. and similar organisations and it is a member of both the Teesside & Sunderland Safety Group. Sillars Holdings is justifiably proud of the very low turnover of staff, who in return pay the Group the best compliments they can by giving long and loyal service, which is very much appreciated.

Above: Modern technology re- surfacing roads.
Below: Sillars offices in 1998.

The quality of drinking water

Hartlepool Gas and Water Company was formed in 1846. The original company, as its name suggests, also supplied gas. Local businessmen appreciated that pure water would promote the health and comfort of the approximately 10,000 inhabitants of the town.

The newly formed company had a chairman and ten directors. It was established as a private company by an act of Parliament and the first source of water was a single cylinder steam engine pump which delivered 40,000 litres of water an hour from a site in Brougham Terrace behind the present Hartlepool Water offices.

To begin with the average consumption of water was less than 20 litres a head a day, at a cost of 1p a cubic metre. Around six miles of main were needed to supply the Headland, West Hartlepool and Seaton Carew with water.

Right: J. A. West, Chairman, circa 1847-1868.
Below: Keeping an eye on the pressure gauge, the old pumping station at Lancaster Road.

Global warming, which means less rain, is a big concern to the company. In addition, the Environment Act 1995, imposed on water companies a new legal duty to promote the efficient use of water by customers. Staff therefore measure very accurately the lowest flow at night into an area. After allowing for customers' night use, the rest is accounted for as leakage. such tests mean the company can concentrate on looking for leaks where leakage is highest.

In 1901 the first town showroom was opened in Church Street. The water supply was extended to Hart in 1903 and land was bought at Howbeck for the sinking of more boreholes. The following year Crookfoot reservoir was formally opened.

New premises were needed and offices were taken in Lancaster Road. (The current offices were built on the same site in the 1970s.) The company's property suffered extensive damage when Hartlepool was bombed in the First World War. The water works were hit but quick repairs made it possible to keep the supply going. Seven employees were wounded and one killed. The government paid £7,500 for bombardment damage.

In the second war, shortage of men was more of a problem though gas and water mains were damaged on 19 occasions. However, the supply of gas and water was never cut off.

The company's main customers are householders, businesses and industry in the Hartlepool area. The core business supplies high quality potable water. In the nineties, Hartlepool Water PLC is still a private company. When publicly owned water authorities were privatised, HW remained an independent company. Today it successfully meets the most stringent health requirements, supplying pure and wholesome water to 92,000 inhabitants in the town.

The company has 20 boreholes on 11 sites stretching from near Darlington to Dalton Piercy. They pump up to three million litres of water an hour and the cost of metered water has only risen to between 37.64p and 43.75p per cubic metre, one of the lowest in the country. The average consumption now is around 150 litres a head each day, supplied through 310 miles of main.

In 1997 Hartlepool Water was acquired by the Anglian Water Group of Companies.

A Business development Team was established at the beginning of 1998. Recently, Hartlepool has taken the lead, within the water industry, to offer a further utility alternative, following the lead of the gas and electricity sectors. The company has launched a new logo as it aims to become the industrial customers' first choice in North East England.

The Business Development Section offers water supply, water treatment, wastewater treatment and support services. Small-business-style customer care is backed by the technical capability and financial muscle of a large multinational parent.

Above: Hartlepool Water's site around the early 1960's.
Below: Today technology takes a part in the quality of our water, (Geographical Information System below).

Engineering manufacturers

Probably one of the most successful Companies in Hartlepool over the past 30 years has been H Q Engineering Ltd who, since their formation by Ted Horsley, Cliff and Gus Quenet in 1965 when they were based in what could best be described as a shed at Central Dock have continually expanded their facilities right up to the present day and for the past 20 years have been carrying out all types of machining, fabrication and engineering contracts both locally and nationally and are now one of the best equipped privately owned Engineering Companies in the North East.

During the late 60's and early 70's the main activity was ship repairs and larger marine engineering contracts which were carried out for all leading shipping companies. This work was always varied and unpredictable and it is great testament to the willingness and loyalty of their workforce that they were always ready to turn out, day and night, usually in atrocious weather conditions to provide a first class round-the-clock service, so essential for this work.

Marine engineering covered all classes of work, ashore and afloat, ranging in size from supplying one bolt to a ship in Union Dock to a full riding squad to complete the installation of a turbo-alternator unit weighing four tonnes during passage of a ship from Redcar Ore Terminal to Tenerife. At least this was the plan and the men were rather disappointed to finish well ahead of

Above: First machine shop in 1972.
Below: Ted Horsley at the controls.

schedule and find themselves set ashore at Immingham instead of Santa Cruz!

In 1973, H Q Engineering carried out the first sea fastening and load out in Hartlepool for the now extremely prosperous North Sea Offshore Oil industry and, although they pioneered a lot of the technology involved in this work, the sheer speed with which this industry grew meant that most of the larger multinational oil companies took over and nowadays, their involvement is confined to the occasional emergency machining contract.

In 1975, the largest shipment of its kind ever to leave Hartlepool by sea was loaded and secured by H Q Engineering. This comprised a giant barge carrying two rock cutting dredgers and five miles of floating pipeline and pontoons, bound for Bahrain in the Persian Gulf and this contract required the Company's welders and riggers to work day and night at Victoria Dock in January - certainly not the warmest place in England.

During most of the 1980's one of the most exciting and prestigious projects to be undertaken in Hartlepool was the total restoration of HMS Warrior which was originally built in 1860 and was the oldest floating iron clad battleship in the world. Although the bulk of the restoration work was done in Jackson Dock, H Q Engineering were involved in the manufacture of numerous replacement parts, some of which were actually made from the few original

always been aware of the need to secure a sound craft base, particularly with the recent decline in the traditional industries in this area and they have always insisted in providing traditional craft apprenticeships since they first started in business. The 12 craft trainees (now called "modern apprentices") which are presently receiving a comprehensive grounding in all areas of Engineering including fabrication, welding, fitting, turning and the operation of heavier machine tools such as borers and planers will hopefully ensure that H Q Engineering don't suffer from any "skills shortage" in the future.

H Q Engineering has, for the past decade been at the forefront of materials reclamation technology and was one of the first companies in the North East to recognise the environmental and commercial advantages to be gained from recycling and preserving existing resources instead of simply destroying and replacing them, Since I 985 they have been one of the leading U.K. manufacturers of Car Flatteners, together with a complete range of steel, scrap and waste processing plant and equipment and have recently opened a dedicated repair and refurbishment facility within their workshops to provide an even

drawings which had somehow survived for 120 years, but most were made from what remaining pieces were available and also from research which the Warrior's design team had carried out. The largest item which was made was a replica of the ship's unique two bladed propellor. It was 26 ft. in diameter and, although it was fabricated from steel plate weighing three tonnes, it was still five times lighter than the original item.

H Q Engineering also manufactured a huge replica crankshaft for the rebuilt engine, together with boiler fronts, smoke doors and thousands of dummy rivet heads. Unfortunately, when completed HMS Warrior was relocated at Portsmouth where sadly it appears to have suffered from a lack of tender loving care, but it will always remain as confirmation of the traditional engineering skills which have still survived in Hartlepool.

HMS Trincomalee is currently undergoing a similar transformation in Harlepool's Historic Quay, as has the Wingfield Castle and, once again H Q Engineering's expertise is regularly called upon to assist the restorers.

Although the main areas of H Q Engineering's investment has always been in machine tools and generally improving their workshop facilities, they have

better service for designing, manufacturing and maintaining the above machinery.

Despite the recent retirement of the founding directors, H Q Engineering are continuing to go from strength to strength with an unchanged management team and are confident that, with the-same positive outlook which they have shown since 1965, they will carry on providing in unrivalled Engineering Service to local, national and international Companies well into the next century.

Above left: Swan-neck crane being demolished in the 1970's.
Bottom: H Q Engineering as it is today.

A family firm where quality counts

Greylin Engineering was set up by Lawrence Inman in 1976. A former ICI employee, he obtained premises at Graythorpe which had formerly been an RAF camp and the company began to establish itself in precision and general engineering, serving the chemical, steelmaking, offshore, brewing, textile and electrical industries.

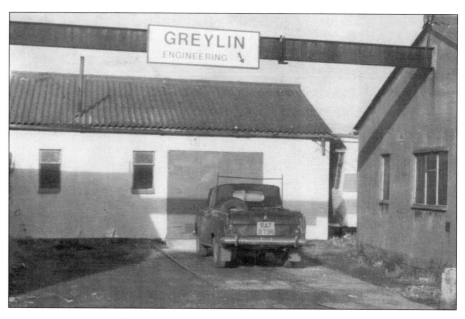

By 1983 the company had grown sufficiently to need new premises and a move was made to the town's Toft Farm Industrial Estate. Lawrence's son Ken was already well established in the firm, having come to it in 1977 and in 1984 Richard Inman, grandson of the founder, joined it too.

In the early nineties, with Ken Inman now the managing director, the company was anxious to demonstrate its commitment to quality. In 1990 it received a fortuitous letter from Hartlepool Enterprise Agency, giving information about a one-day seminar entitled, 'Introducing Quality Standards. The company was represented on the course and made good use of the information on offer. It also contacted and received valuable help from the Department of Trade and Industry. Advice was also taken from consultants Touche Ross of Newcastle.

to match components exactly to customer requirements.

Not a company to rest on its laurels, Greylin is constantly upgrading its machinery and its procedures and looks forward to further qualifications and more satisfied customers in the next millennium.

Above: The modern day engineering process.
Top left: Three generations of Greylin. From left to right are Ken Inman, Lawrence Inman and Richard Inman.
Facing page, top: The original premises at Greythorpe.
Facing page, bottom: The presentation of the BS 5750 Certificate to Kenneth Inman (MD).
Below: Part of the modern fleet.

BS 5750 became Greylin Engineering's aim and the whole work force made every effort to achieve it quickly.

Councillor Bob Barnfather, Chairman of the Council's economic development committee, was pleased to be able to present part 2 of the BS 5750 certificate to Greylin Engineering Ltd in April 1992. This was the year that saw the birth of the open European market, which the company entered with an accredited indication of its ability in forward thinking which caused them to apply for it in the first place and in quality which enabled them to achieve it.

Now the company has also achieved ISO 9002. Its customers include British Steel, Nuclear Electrics, Clydesdale Forge, Seal Electrical and many other well known firms. They attribute their success to taking the trouble

Local service with national standards

At the turn of the century a legal partnership, Turnbull & Tilly, practised in Hartlepool. They had a long history as Notaries Public dealing with Shipmasters' claims and were based in the same office at 13, Church Street in which Edward Turnbull had originally started his practice in 1841.

The original Mr Tilly took his eldest son into the partnership and the firm continued until Mr Tilly senior's death in 1932. The firm was then expanded by amalgamation with two other local firms. As Temperley, Tilly & Hayward, it moved to larger offices in Church Street, opposite Turnbull's first premises.

Tilly's two of great grandsons are partners in the present firm of Tilly, Bailey & Irvine, making them the fourth generation of the family to practise as solicitors in Hartlepool and to continue the family's 130 year history of providing legal services in the town.

Meanwhile, in 1949, Mr J B Irvine, the son of a West Hartlepool timber merchant, entered into partnership with F W J Webb. Mr Webb, had been practising with Edward Fryer, a firm established in 1897. As Fryer, Webb & Irvine, the new partnership continued until 1955. Then it amalgamated with Harry Bailey & Son, becoming Webb, Bailey & Irvine. The latter practice worked in association with Temperley, Tilly & Hayward amalgamating in 1969, forming the present firm of Tilly, Bailey & Irvine of York Chambers, York Road, Hartlepool.

It is remarkable that, last century, at a time of great prosperity in Hartlepool, the present firm's predecessors operated with two partners and a small supporting staff. Now, when the town is alleged to be depressed and poorer, its position is maintained with fourteen partners and sixteen other solicitors with half a dozen executives, plus typists, accountants, receptionists and a whole battery of complicated machines.

The administration of the law has become vastly more complicated. In addition, what is today regarded as poverty would have been counted affluence a hundred years ago.

Over the years, Tilly, Bailey & Irvine has developed to meet the changing needs of the locality. In the early days, much of its expertise was in the traditional north-eastern industries of coal, shipping and steel. Today, whilst remaining one of the leading northern firms in the field of shipping, it is geared to the fast-changing business environment of the 1990s.

TILLY'S TWO GREAT GRANDSONS ARE STILL PARTNERS IN THE PRESENT FIRM OF TILLY BAILEY & IRVINE.

The staff works closely with its clients as part of the business management team, helping them to achieve their own targets by making the best use of the firm's resources. Backed up by the latest technology and skilled personnel, Tilly,

Bailey & Irvine offers a fast, responsive service to its substantial client base which ranges from private clients to many public companies and authorities.

The firm offers a full investment management and stockbroking service. The Investment Department is staffed by experienced investment management personnel, and supervised by a partner authorised by the Law society to deal in securities and portfolios.

The firm is one of only a few in the north which offers an 'in house' town planning service to its clients, run by a Chartered Town Planner with extensive local Council experience. All this is in addition to a full range of traditional legal services. The practice places great emphasis on the traditional values of courtesy, integrity and friendliness. It combines this with modern office technology to provide clients with a service which is swift, cost-effective and personal to them.

Left: Harry Bailey. ***Facing page:*** *Tobias Harry Tilly senior.* ***Below:*** *John Tilly with Peter Mandelson M. D. outside the firm's premises.*

Servicing the building industry since 1860

James Atkinson, born in 1808 of a yeoman farming family in Westmorland, went into partnership with his son James Thomas, to form the origins of the present company, then known as J. Atkinson & Son, Slaters, Tilers and Slate Merchants in Darlington. He would have been surprised to hear that the fifth and sixth generations of his family would still be actively involved in its management more than a century and a quarter later.

Thomas Atkinson died at the early age of 42, leaving his son James Thornton Atkinson in charge in the early years of this century. His father had opened new branches in Spennymoor and Hartlepool. James junior worked hard, slating by day and doing the office work by night. By 1904 the firm was worth the considerable sum of £5,000 and owned several houses taken in payment for bad debts. The firm prospered, taking over two Darlington businesses, a slaters and a builders merchant.

In 1925 a limited company was formed, James Thornton and his two sons James and George being the directors. The business expanded further between the wars. A new branch in Bridge Road, Stockton enabled slates to be shipped via the River Tees directly from Wales. Interesting jobs in those years included covering the then new Faverdale Wagon Works, at Darlington with more than a million Welsh slates and, in 1939, covering the roofs of barrage balloon hangars in Northumberland with some six acres of asbestos cement roofing sheets.

In 1950 a riverside yard and roofing stocks were acquired in Stockton, where the present site was bought in 1965. The same year marked the opening of the Bedale branch.

Above left: James Atkinson, born in 1808 and founder of the company.
Below: A photograph of the company's showroom at Park Road, Hartlepool taken about 1922.

Merchant in Penrith. This extended the trading area to include the birth place of the founder.

Currently the family management is in its sixth generation. The company is still looking to increase its share of the building material and home improvement market. They also make sure that today's customers are offered the same family service that those of earlier generations learned to expect.

With eleven branches covering every corner of the North East England and a further depot in Penrith, Atkinsons provide a first class service to anyone concerned with building or home improvement.

Top: Atkinson's Park Road Premises in 1975. Left: The financial director, Bernard Atkinson in the early days. Below: A 1940 calendar issued by the company.

In 1973, Senior Director James Atkinson died. He had joined the company in 1918 as an apprentice slater and the progressive development of the builders merchant side of the company was largely due to him. Away from the business, he was chairman of the Hartlepool Building Society and founder member and Commodore of the Hartlepool Yacht Club. During his career the company made 16 takeovers and introduced plumbers merchanting and the Tools & Tackle Division.

In 1975 a branch opened in Northallerton, enabling the company to provide a much better service to the Dales. Two years later the Plumbing and Heating Departments moved from Park Road to new purpose-built warehouses and offices in Burn Road, Hartlepool.

In 1985 the company celebrated its 125th anniversary aboard HMS Warrior, the world's first iron-clad battleship, also 125 years old and then being restored in Hartlepool harbour.

An important step was taken in 1991 when the company acquired Thomas Althams a Builders

The business under the clock

Henry Lamb established his business in Lynn Street, West Hartlepool in 1873. On a flier, published in the early days, he described himself as a "Practical Watchmaker, Jeweller, Silversmith and Optician." Furthermore, "Every description of Repairs" were "executed upon the premises at moderate charges.

According to the illustrations, this included repairs to microscopes, telescopes and spectacles. A ribbon banner reminded customers that 'Time is money'.

Since then three generations of the Lambs family have run the business in turn, Matthew taking over from Henry and Harry from Matthew. The Lynn Street premises served them well until as late as 1969. They served too as an official meteorological station and figures were published in the Hartlepool Mail under the headline, 'Mr H Lamb's Barometer'. The barometer referred to is still in use.

The business continued through the two world wars. During these years the shop opened only one day a week and continued to serve customers although with a limited stock.

The clock that hung above the premises and made the shop easy to find was a well known local rendezvous. Many romances started with a meeting 'under the clock' and often resulted in the purchase of a wedding ring from the Lambs' large stock.

Above: An advertisement taken from an early trades journal. Below: Lynn Street at the turn of the century. The business moved from here in 1969.

Customers soon became used to shopping at Lambs' new home and the business continues to have loyal local customer base. Many who have moved away, even abroad, still return to them. They appreciate the very personal service and the individual, high quality jewellery designs.

Lambs is still a totally independent family-run business and it continues to repair as well as sell clocks, watches and jewellery. Some of the work is still effected in their own workshops. The family hopes to serve Hartlepool customers for many years to come.

Left: Lamb's shop in 1938.
Bottom left: The clock, in Lynn Street. Below: Harry Lamb outside the Lynn Street shop in October 1962.

This clock had to be moved in May 1969, when the business moved its home to 116 York Road. It was difficult to remove and relocate it and also to transfer some of the shops original solid mahogany wall cases and cabinets.

The company with a global reputation

Supaflo Engineering began its operations in Hartlepool almost 25 years ago. The company was a breakaway from Darchem Engineering in Stillington, County Durham. In the early years the firm established itself as a leading manufacturer of butt weld pipe fittings. It rapidly became known as a reliable and competitive supplier throughout the petrochemical, nuclear, gas and oil industries.

During the eighties the company became part of the RMH Group of Companies, a Midlands-based operation. Supaflo is now a sister company of SSE Pipefittings Ltd of Dudley, West Midlands. With the added strength and support of this Group, Supaflo Engineering has made significant advances, both in the UK and on the export front.

The Hartlepool operation makes cold extrusion presses up to 500 tonnes capacity, capable of cold forming 8" NB elbows with a wall thickness of

0.9" with great accuracy. They use the finest materials and offer a speedy and efficient service this being a crucial part of the firm's efforts to satisfy their customers.

Supaflo is proud of being a Hartlepool company and the Renaissance of the town and area means that it can look to the future with increasing optimism.

Supaflo Engineering shares a close working relationship with many other local companies and organisations, including the local College of Further Education. Supaflo has recently taken on young people as Modern Apprentices.

The company is frequently audited and approved by numerous standards authorities, including NQA, Dienst voor het Stoomwezen, TUV and BNFL. Their quality system fully meets the requirements of BS EN ISO 9002: 1994.

The management team is determined that, as the company nears its 25th anniversary, its success story will continue into the next millennium.

Above: The factory:
Left: The office staff.
Top left: Some of the engineers.

An extra-ORD-inary business

When Benjamin Thomas Ord set up his printing and stationery business in Northgate in 1840 the town of 'West' Hartlepool did not exist. The opening of the West Dock several years later and the rapid development of the new town no doubt had great benefits for his operations.

The expansion developed for the remainder of the 19th century to a point where a base in the new town became a priority and premises were obtained at 9-11 Tower Street.

B. T. Ord, as the business was called at that time, continued to produce printed matter and stationery for the thriving iron, coal and timber trades in South West Durham as well as for countless local businesses.

Such was the demand that around 1930 the company obtained additional workshops at 3-7 Tower Street, a building formerly occupied by Ewart Parsons Ltd.

Three generations of Benjamin Thomas Ord's guided the firm from its beginnings and up to 1989 when the last 'Bertie' Ord passed away.

The firm was then bought by another local printers - E W Harrison & Son Ltd who amalgamated the businesses to continue to trade under the ORDS banner.

Although the services of the company have changed little through the past 150 years, the technology employed has changed beyond all recognition.

All services today are computer driven and controlled, with modern offset litho and digital printing presses employed to give speed and quality to the customer.

The retail premises in Tower Street offers a wide selection of stationery, office furniture and consumables; while printing and administration is located in a modern, single-storey factory on Usworth Road Industrial Estate.

Although the Ord family are no longer involved, their original philosophy of offering top quality service at affordable prices remains the company policy as it approaches its 160th birthday at the start of the new millennium.

Below: The Tower Street printing office, circa 1900.

It began with a home made bus

Before 1920, Thomas Richardson, generally known as 'Tot', was a butcher's boy. In that year, together with his brothers, Arthur and Bill, he set himself up in the transport business.

He started by buying a truck. Then his grandfather, John Richardson, not a member of the firm but a joiner in his own right, built a body to fit on to the back of the truck to turn it into a charabanc.

At their premises in Oxford Road, Tot served the business as the engineer. Arthur was the organiser, deciding destinations, advertising trips and generally overseeing the firm's activities. Bill did the driving.

By 1949 business had increased so that further premises on Oxford Road were taken. This new site had been the old Howcrofts' Fairground equipment factory where carousels etc were built. Richardsons' operations were run from the two sites.

Temporary setbacks were experienced when shipyards closed and the power station was built but otherwise the company steadily grew. Richardsons was very busy during the war years taking the munitions factory hands to work. When air raids struck, the company's drivers would move its vehicles out of the yard where they were usually stored to make sure they were not all damaged at the same time.

Today Richardsons still offer the Hartlepool public a private hire service, long distance if required. Customers are loyal, appreciating that the company's service has a personal touch and is backed by a sound local knowledge. Now run by David Richardson, (the third generation). The family is looking forward to transporting Hartlepool into the next millennium.

Above: One of the coaches in the mid 1940's.
Below: A thriving company Richardson's today.
Bottom: In and outside the bus in the late 1940's.

A touch of luxury

In 1975, Geoffrey Bassett, who owned and worked in a London concern, All Blinds & Shutters, took premises in York Road, Hartlepool. There, his girl friend, Dianne Lithgo, now Mrs Bassett, with the assistance of three other ladies, made curtains for the London company.

At first, this work was carried out on standard flat machines. Now they use overlockers and blind stitch machines that gives results that look like hand sewing. The work was begun purely as an outlet for All Blinds & Shutters as manufacturing outlets were not easily come by. Because of by by-laws the front of the building had to be kept as a retail outlet. Rolls of fabric were therefore put in the window and if customers came in, their orders were a bonus. There was a sewing machine in the shop so that the London work could proceed as Dianne waited for Hartlepool customers. Geoff commuted - and still does - between London and Hartlepool, installing curtains for local clients when he was in Cleveland.

Local work expanded, so that when the next-door Italian furniture shop closed Contessa bought it and expanded into it. The directors at Contessa attribute their success to offering the customer a touch of luxury and the benefit of Geoff's London experience which ensures that their stock includes the new fashions as soon as they are available.

The store is laid out with around 20 window-sized displays which show clients the variety of work it is possible for Contessa to carry out. Books of samples contain fabrics ranging from plain and simple to exclusive printed silk.

No written guarantee is offered because, on the rare occasions a customer has some complaint, Contessa Curtains like to make personal restitution to the complainant and to settle the occasional problem in a friendly way.

The company is one of the largest independent curtain retailers in the area. Dianne and Geoff have been joined as directors by David Burmiston who began work for them 15 years ago on a YTS scheme. As a group, they are committed to maintaining their high standards and are looking to the areas surrounding Hartlepool to expand their business.

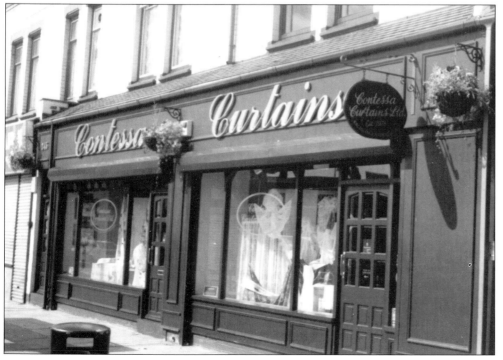

Top: A view of the shop in the 1970's.
Above left: How the shop used to look in the 1970's.
Left: Contessa today.

Vicarage Gardens in a picture dating from 1966

ACKNOWLEDGMENTS

DRP FERRIDAY

HARTLEPOOL BOROUGH LIBRARIES

HARTLEPOOL MAIL

ELIZABETH LAW

THE NORTHERN ECHO